NEIL CAMERON has directed theatre and arts events with the community for over twenty years and in that time has produced eighty four major productions. He has worked mainly in England, Scotland and Australia but also in Japan, Holland, Germany, Canada, USA and New Zealand. Two of his productions have won the 'Event of the Year' in the Northern Territory and he was also the director of the Melbourne Peace Vigil Festival which won a United Nations Peace Award for Australia.

He came to Melbourne as a Gulbenkian Scholarship recipient in 1981 and has lived in Australia since then. He is well known for his large scale ceremonies which include community involvement and large and spectacular visual effects using fire, music and fireworks. These events have been presented to over 60,000 people in the last two years.

Neil Cameron travels widely lecturing on theatre in the community and lives in Maleny, Queensland.

This book is dedicated to all the artists and members of the community who have given their time, talents and enthusiasm.

CURRENCY DRAMATISTS SERIES
General Editor: MARGARET WILLIAMS

Stephen Sewell: The Playwright as Revolutionary
— *Peter Fitzpatrick*
Dorothy Hewett: The Feminine as Subversion
— *Margaret Williams*
Community Theatre in Australia
— *Richard Fotheringham* (ed.)

FIRE
ON THE
WATER

**A personal view
of theatre in the
community**

NEIL CAMERON

Currency Press • Sydney

First published in 1993 by
Currency Press Pty Ltd,
PO Box 452 Paddington
NSW 2021, Australia

National Library of Australia
Cataloguing-in-Publication data

Cameron, Neil 1946-
Fire on the water

Bibliography
ISBN 0 86819 307 0

1.Community theatre. I.Title. (Series: Currency
dramatists series).

792.022

Currency's creative writing program is
assisted by the Australia Council, the
Federal Government's arts funding and
advisory body.

Cover Design by Trevor Hood
Set by Currency, Paddington
Printed by Southwood Press, Marrickville NSW

CONTENTS

∎

'I believe the theatre to be a communal project, a celebration. It is a form of expression that will become more and more a necessity as society becomes increasingly mechanical and organised. Theatre is a way to get people to communicate with each other, to destroy the walls which make us separate ... People are sad because they have lost their animality, their sense of play. With modern civilisation man has become a spectator. Theatre should be a feast, a joyous occasion, a festival.'

Jerome Savary, The Grand Magic Circus,
quoted in James Roose-Evans,
Experimental Theatre from Stanislavsky to Peter Brook

When I first contemplated writing this book Wendy Lowenstein said, 'I think you should, but it will take several years.' She was right and in the end it took five years. All through that time people have given me support and I would like to thank them all, especially Faridah Whyte, Winsome McCaughey and the Riechstein Trust, Michael Liffman and the Myer Foundation, the Community and Cultural Development Unit of the Australia Council, Jan (Meme) McDonald, Sandra Gorman.

N.C.

INTRODUCTION

■

'Up here, spectator!'

After the Russian Revolution in 1917 the great Russian theatre director Myerhold was attempting to reach his audience in new revolutionary ways and to break through the 'invisible wall' that separates the performers from the spectator: to make theatre part of the worker's lives. He was an amazing innovator. He was breaking down the idea of the proscenium arch stage, which he believed was stultifying, and developing the use of circus tricks, acrobatics, swivelling stages, theatre in the round and open air performances which included thousands of actors. A wonderful example of his flair and determination was a theatre piece aptly named 'The Storming of the Winter Palace' which was played to one hundred thousand people in Leningrad. He used 8000 people in the cast, a musical section of 500, fireworks, cannon fire from the Aurora battleship and three separate theatre areas. He ran the show from a stage in the middle of the action with flare and motorcycle signals.

In 1921 in the last scene of his production of Mayakovsky's 'Mystery Bouffe' he shocked critics by inviting the audience to climb onto the stage and join with the performers in community based celebration. His cry was 'Up here, spectator!' It was a symbolic gesture, an invitation for actors and members of the community to come together, to make theatre live within the wider community.

The philosophy inherent in those early revolutionary days, and one so deeply reflected in the views of Brecht, was that culture was for the people and the artist's job was to work towards an integration of culture and the citizen. Theatre should be an integrated part of people's lives and not a specialist pursuit of the few. To achieve integration one had to break down the very form of existing theatre and find new ways to write, design, act and present the work; to break out of convention and go 'through theatre back into life,' as Artaud said.

Mayakovsky's methods worked and his theatre became a vital force in the society in which he lived and his work was indeed popular with the 'people,' so much so that he was to die in Stalin's death camps as the rise of totalitarianism crushed individual and community expression.

In the seventy years that followed, directors, actors, writers and theatre workers of all kinds experimented with a popular theatre, the evolution of a theatre which was essential in people's lives, a theatre which combats the mechanised consumer culture of the twentieth century, one which helps us celebrate and understand our existence, one which frightens us and wakes us up. It is a theatre which has given voice to dissension, focused protest and articulated social and political ideals and yet it has also given us new directions, clearer paths and provided vision for the future. It has struggled to express the deepest feelings about being alive.

I believe that theatre must do this if it is to stay vibrant and relevant. This is the very excitement of theatre, the very reason for it and where its essential energy lies.

Around 1970, Grotowski reorganised his company, took some young people with no previous professional theatrical experience, and worked to develop a means of leading participants back into the elemental connections between people and their bodies, imagination, the natural world and each other.

                        History of the Theatre, Oscar Brockett

Part of this experimental development has been the abandonment of the purpose-built theatre space and the creation of theatre with the spectator, with the community. The results have been exciting both artistically and socially in countries all over the world. Peter Brook has said that theatre is a necessity in our lives. The arts have always been central to our understanding of ourselves. The expression in many and varied forms of our inner and external lives, our spiritual beings and our society, have been essential for human growth. Yet when ordinary people in modern industrial countries think of theatre they imagine a world of make-up, curtains, lights, stage and props inhabited by strange, slightly decadent actors. It is not a world for them and indeed most people rarely visit it. Many have never even been inside a theatre.

New forms of theatre have broken down these attitudes and theatre has become a part of many communities. It has broken through the walls of purpose-built theatre spaces and reached the wider world. It is a theatre which has gone back to its beginnings to make theatre work again for society as a whole.

It has adapted thousands of years of tradition, which has sustained theatre through the ages, to new purposes and new directions. It has looked to pagan ceremonies, strolling players, Greek theatre, commedia dell'arte, music hall, circus, religious ritual, buskers, open air theatre, cabaret and fairgrounds for its inspiration and it has looked to the community for its motivation. It is theatre in circus tents, pubs, churches, streets, trams, boats, schools, parades, festivals and a thousand other places where people naturally gather. In Australia it is in fact the foundation of a new theatre tradition, lively and relevant in its own place and time, and is also about giving theatre back to the people at large and inviting them to practise it as a form of ritual, communication, expression, celebration, entertainment and comment. This book aims to describe the effect theatre has on individuals and on different types of communities as they regain access to the arts and of the profound power that theatre has to focus ideas, concepts and visions.

Communities can be defined by geographical location, ethnic group, age, living conditions or shared beliefs and in any number of other ways, but certain conditions hold true to each. The individual members feel a common identity and see themselves as part of a defined group. They know its language, its habits, its beliefs and its relationship to themselves; in other words they know its culture and feel part of it.

The forms of community theatre are as varied as the communities themselves. It can take the form of a play either inside or out, a professional theatre group touring a show, street theatre, a community celebration of any other of the hundreds of forms being practised throughout the country. But every form shares a common thread and that is to help make theatre live again in the daily lives of Australians. It is not a substitute for formal theatre presented in theatres, neither is it there just to develop a formal theatre going audience, it is there for all people to experience and enjoy in whatever form it takes, for its own sake.

Consequently this book is about a journey into the world of possibilities, when theatre moves into an uncharted land, an uncontrolled situation, being swept along by life itself. The book offers blueprints for action

in all sorts of situations and ways in which problems
can be solved. It is also my own journey, which has
taken up the last twenty years of my life and many of
the examples in this book are taken from my own
experience. The journey has been an exciting one and
has given me a wonderful chance to share in other lives
and cultures. It is not then an academic study but
theatre seen through the eyes of one practitioner who
has followed one particular road.

The New World and the Old

Australia is a fascinating and unique country in which
to practise celebratory theatre. In stepping out of the
European-based theatre tradition one needs not be
apprehensive. The theatre worker is not leaving culture
behind and entering some sort of artistic desert but
rather embracing a new and exciting world made up of
challenge and exploration.

Australia is situated in South East Asia. Its
neighbouring cultures produce outstanding sources of
inspiration: the masks of New Guinea, the dancing of
Melanesia, the religious rituals, shadow puppets and
gamelan music of Indonesia and the art of the Maori to
name but a few. The Aboriginal people have the oldest
living culture in the world where we can see if we look
a mode of expression that goes back 35,000 years, in fact
to our own beginnings.

People from all over the world have come to Australia
bringing their own theatre traditions. Their art,
literature, music, dance, and stories are a source of
constant enrichment. From the mix of old and new,
Australian culture is being formed and evolved. The
most exciting aspect to Australian theatre is that it is
free to invent itself.

An historic moment in that cultural evolution
happened in 1983 in the rural setting of Albury-

Wodonga on the border between Victoria and New
South Wales.

Some years before, Peter Oyston had become the first
Dean of Drama at the newly formed Victoria College of
the Arts and had instituted a revolutionary new course
in theatre. It had worked on the basic assumption that
theatre had to be taken out of a theatre-based
environment and placed firmly into the Australian
culture. In the last year of the first intake, Oyston sent
his students out into the world with the suggestion that
they form small regional companies. One of the groups
formed West Theatre Company, where I was later to
work, and another formed the Murray River Performing
Group, based in Albury-Wodonga. Among many other
interesting projects, they formed the Flying Fruit Fly
Circus. Young people were given the chance to work
with professional circus workers. They quickly gained
exceptional skills which thrilled audiences with stunning
displays made even more powerful by the fact that
these were kids from the local community.

In 1983 Carrillo Gantner who had been the artistic
director of the Playbox Theatre in Melbourne had
become cultural attache in China. He helped organise
instructors from the world famous Nanjing Acrobatics to
come to Fruit Fly for a residency of twelve weeks.
Performers from Circus Oz and other interested artists
joined the youngsters for the training. More than sixty
Australians came together with the visiting Asian
instructors for a show at the end of training.

The end result was an astounding evening and I feel
that it was a turning point in Australian culture. The
Chinese discipline and technique showed in the level of
performance which was superlative; the Australians in
their turn had added a sense of vivacious joy to the
whole feeling of the show.

But what we all realised that night was that we had transcended the distinctions of professional and amateur, Chinese and Australian, child and adult and had become something new. At the same time, we realised that Australians could not only perform with the best in the world but also could add something unique to that international experience which could only be explained as 'Australian.' This is the oldest land on earth and yet a new culture must evolve if our people are to grow and expand in a healthy and truthful way which allows a creative and generous way of life.

A New Kind of Theatre Maker

Producing theatre involving the wider community is exciting work, but it pushes creativity to the limit. Theatre practitioners have to come to terms with the challenges that face them when they leave the controlled environment of purpose-built theatres. They must learn to communicate their craft to all sorts of people and communities. They must de-mystify their work and open it up to the lay person and yet still be the creative force behind the productions. They must walk the fine line between being utilised by a community and being used by that community. They are artists and must learn to remain artists but to see themselves as part of a community.

A major part of this new learning is to determine who is creating what for whom. In conventional theatre the differentiation is obvious. The audience's role is to watch and the theatre maker's role to perform the show. These clear deliniations do not exist in a theatre form which has merged into its audience, but theatre can work at every level of involvement if the project is structured in the right way. It takes time, training and experience to learn how to structure this type of theatre.

The training that produces an actor for the stage may not equip the creative theatre worker for producing work outside of that environment. At its core, theatre must be the exploration of the self. Theatre workers must learn these techniques where they, as creators, combine with the voice and talents of the community to express a shared vision. Community theatre is visual, musical; a theatre which often includes fireworks, parades, flags, acrobatics, dance and song. All these facets (and more) must be understood.

Theatre workers must also learn to organise resources and funding and to be able to utilise them in the right way to evolve financial strategies which are going to work in the short and long term. This means mastering methods of fund raising through government and other sources and being able to administer budgets which sometimes run into hundreds of thousands of dollars. Many of these skills and techniques are outlined in this book.

Before the journey begins I would like to explain briefly my own introduction to community theatre and how it affected my life. In 1972 I was attending college in Edinburgh when out of the blue I was asked to help a fellow student who was working in a slum area in the city. She was working with deprived children at an adventure playground in a particularly bad area known as Craigmillar. I went down to help and was deeply shocked by the conditions in which these children were living. It was my first real exposure to poverty as my middle class upbringing had never taken me into this section of my own city. This area had all the classic symptoms of a slum; poor quality housing with smashed windows, leaking roofs and old grey paint; high unemployment which led to poverty and therefore crime and few facilities to help resource the area. It was shocking to see the misery that people were living in, in my own country, in the affluent West.

After some weeks the leader of the playground asked me to run drama lessons which he felt would be successful. I had no idea what drama lessons were but was eager to try anything which might help. I went to Theatre Workshop in Edinburgh and was taught the basics by the director, Reg Bolton. Within weeks the drama classes in Craigmillar had really taken off, with young people coming from the poorest homes. It was obvious even to me, with no drama experience, that they were getting a great deal out of it and beginning to build something positive in their lives. I was witnessing, although I did not know it then, the enormous positive power that creativity has on the individual.

Coincidentally, in an old building next door to the playground there was a small and unusual group led by an extraordinary woman called Helen Crummy. As a local mother she had gone to her son's school to arrange for her son to study the violin. Her request was dismissed as ridiculous. The principal said he had enough trouble teaching the children to read and write, let alone learn music. Helen believed that the young people of the area had a right to have access to the arts, especially in a city which ran one of the biggest arts festivals in the world. She and other local women formed the Craigmillar Festival Society which ran a small festival to demonstrate the talents of its youth. A professional theatre director, Sandy Neilson, had become involved by chance as professional involvement in community events was unheard of at that time in Scotland. He directed a show which local people helped write and perform.

I went along to see the show. It was outstanding and quite revolutionary. Given some professional help, the cast put on a show full of vitality, humour, music and passion which would have been very difficult to duplicate in the professional world. The true story concerned a poor woman in the 19th century who had become pregnant to a rich landowner. She had the baby and drowned it in the local river because she was unable to look after it. For her crime she was hanged and her body was carried from the execution area in central Edinburgh to Craigmillar for burial nearby. It was a hot day and the mourners went into the local pub to refresh themselves. Half way through having a drink the hanged woman entered the pub. She had not been killed by the hangman and had recovered enough to rise out of the coffin! Having survived she had another chance at life. The show finished with a song about rebirth and the story became a metaphor for the area's determination to change its own situation and to bring about a new beginning, and it was going to use the arts to do it. Theatre and creativity had become an instrument to bring about change.

It all might have dwindled at this point but for a coincidence. The local Craigmillar councillor became Lord Provost of Edinburgh, which is the equivalent of the city mayor in Australia. He wanted to put new resources into the area and the local festival group seemed the best place to start. But this was only part of the extraordinary equation. The local festival had applied to the anti-poverty program for funds to run a two year rejuvenation plan using the arts as a base and their application was successful. For the first time a slum had been given proper funding to develop a self help program and using the arts as a base.

It was a huge and successful program which eventually employed over one hundred local people who were working in every area of social reform. It was being proven conclusively that the poor can break the cycle of poverty given proper resources and professional help. Helen did not lose her vision about the potential of creativity in each person and used this as the driving philosophy of the organisation. An arts centre was built by local residents from an old church, murals and arts programs were launched, a printing press was set up, events and festivals organised and large scale environmental improvements made, all organised through the energy of the local people. This all linked to job creation, social services, legal help, communication and planning as well as programs for the handicapped, the aged and the young. It became very effective and was bringing hope and change to the area. So successful was it that other areas in Scotland began to follow the model including Glasgow's Easterhouse Festival which was later to become very well known. The whole development was being researched by Edinburgh University and the E.E.C. Poverty Fund who were very interested in the success of an arts program in this context.

I had become involved with the Festival Society and had become the Arts Director working alongside local people. The climax to several years' work came when we were invited to Holland and Belgium to perform a show as part of the poverty funds program.

We put together a review of many of the highlights of the shows that had been produced. A cast of forty-five was brought together, comprising people who had very rarely left the Craigmillar area.

Over the years the situation in Craigmillar had changed from people living in helpless poverty into a group who were able to take social action in their own right. The politics of this situation are interesting, but for me there was equal excitement in the art product they were producing. It was full of energy, life and passion: a truly living theatre.

The show was very successful with packed houses
every night on the tour, but the truly magical moment
came when we arrived at the village which was to host
us. We got out of the bus just outside the village limits
and decided to march into town in a procession led by
the bagpipes. The Dutch people lined the streets
cheering and clapping, but also they were weeping and
seemed very emotional. We were taken to the village
hall and it was packed with local people. The local
mayor welcomed us and we discovered that it had been
a Scottish regiment that had freed the village after Nazi
occupation and the first sound of freedom the villagers
had heard was the sound of the bagpipes.

It was a moving experience. As I looked around the
room I could see the Craigmillar people filled with
pride. The struggle to understand life and the power to
express and overcome its difficulties lay within the arts;
this thought had somehow crystallised within us all.

There was no doubt in my mind over those years of
work that the arts and theatre in particular could bring
about change in the individual and society itself and
how exciting it was to be an artist who helped to enable
the release of that power.

Community theatre is a growing force in Australia.
More and more artists are going out into the
mainstream of society to work with people from all
walks of life, our open air and street theatre is reaching
international quality, parades, rituals and festivals are
using artists to deepen their meaning and theatre
workers of all kinds are developing new ways to
communicate and express our culture. I hope this book
will help students, artists and communities to want to
practice this form of theatre and that it will be useful to
the thousands of people throughout the country who
are already involved.

                                                    Maleny, 1993

■

PART ONE

Street Theatre and Open Air Performance

Professional theatre makers taking
theatre out of formal theatre spaces and
into society

ONE

■

Back to the Beginning

It is anti-authoritarian, anti-traditional, anti-pomp anti-pretence ... it is of noise and the theatre of noise, it is the theatre of applause ... It feeds on the deep and true aspirations in the audience and taps infinite resources of energy ... Salt, sweat, noise and smell: the theatre that's not in a theatre, the theatre on carts, on wagons, on trestles, audiences standing ... audiences joining in, answering back.

PETER BROOK

Looking Back

It has often been this 'rough' theatre as Brook described it which has survived through times when other forms of theatre have died. It is the rascally cousin of formal presentation and has always sided with the common people. It has been the theatre of the traveller, the mountebank, the clown, the storyteller, the fairground. Without props or much scenery it has persisted through persecution, war, plague and famine. It is the perpetual link between different forms of theatre in different cultures and different times and that rough quality must be seen as its delight in life in the raw, at the base and heart of things.

Fire and Drums—Tribal Theatre

This theatre is one of the oldest forms of art. Ancient tribal groups would gather around the fire, listen to the drums and hear the stories of the hunt or the adventures of their gods. This was no light entertainment. The theatre of the time related vital information to the tribes about their history and ancestors. In an age without the written word, theatre was one of the vital channels of information exchange. This information moved human beings from a purely day to day existence to understanding that the experiences of the past could help in planning the future. This handing on of knowledge vital to the tribe's survival, in time could become sacred. The information also became synonymous with the identity of the group and the artists who depicted the art had a huge influence on the group's view of itself. The theatre became the tribe's vision of its own beliefs and in so doing had a deep effect on what those beliefs were.

Therefore, the practice of performance was in the hands of the shaman, priest or witch doctor who harnessed the tribe's spiritual aspirations and channelled its creativity. Theatre expressed their understanding of the world about them and it was natural that the process, the theatre act itself, should become filled with that same sense of magic. In the portrayal of the deities, the power of the hunt or the victory over enemies, the actors could imaginatively summon up these forces and lead the tribe to the source of life. The theatre makers

would at times become stage managers of huge events
which involved the whole village in a manifestation of
this power. The tribe would dance and sing for many
hours, sometimes days at a time, sending the
participants into trance and ecstasy, nearer to the gods.
These ceremonies would celebrate the seasons or
important occasions such as initiation or death. The role
of theatre was closely wrapped up in religion,
celebration, education and ritual and was central to the
tribe's way of life.

We can speculate that laughter as well as admiration
was a part of these performances, when humour became
a safety valve to the high drama. Some of the actors
would mimic the seriousness of their own activities and
reflect the more ordinary activities of the tribe. They
would act out the scandals and love affairs and defuse
the pompous and the powerful. By these means they
handed on another level of history and understanding
which is equally important to the human condition, our
ability to laugh at ourselves. Over the centuries the
functions of religion and theatre separated and the
priest and theatre maker parted company. The tribal
way of life was changing as the population increased
and the deep relationship between people and the soil
weakened.

This kind of theatre is still a powerful force today in
Indonesia and parts of Asia where they celebrate local
languages in festivals where national pressures
endanger their survival.

Formal Theatre

As population grew, so too did the audience. The simple
circle of villagers sitting around the actors became
inadequate and more effective ways to set up spaces
became a necessity. These new audiences were now

becoming observers rather than participants in their theatre. A problem arose: how could the larger audience continue to hear and see? The answer was straightforward. Either the actor was put on a dais or the audience was put on a slope. The ancient Greeks devised the semi-circular amphitheatre which provided excellent acoustics for up to 14,000 people, and later the Romans elaborated on this design. Because the space was now fairly controlled, external noise and audience movement was less of a problem. But these new and infinitely more sophisticated arenas demanded the development of a new range of techniques.

The voice now had to reach a much larger audience and gesture was developed to convey meaning to people who were a long way off. But this formalisation of performance developed its own theatre style and gone was the intimacy between performer and audience. With village theatre the audience and actor were part of the same close knit social group, but with the development of city life the actors and audience were to start to separate from one another.

The Greek and Roman Empires fell but theatre did not die. Travelling performers and story tellers kept it alive from village to village; in China there were shamanistic rituals, clowns, jugglers and puppet shows. By the 12th century song and story had developed into a flourishing traditional theatre in which audiences stood around a stage six feet high (about two metres) and heard tales of emperors, courtesans, heroes and peasants, presented in formal dialogue, song and dance. In Europe the Christian church provided the next great movement of drama around the fourteenth century, when the drama of praise and thanksgiving which took place in the monastic churches gradually developed into a method of teaching the scriptures. These were to become the medieval Miracle Cycles and Morality Plays which were performed outside the church in streets and marketplaces and became associated with the northern hemisphere summer festival. Over the centuries the performances became more elaborate and in England the trade guilds began to finance and carry out productions. The distance between religious and secular performance grew as did the size of the audiences and in the late sixteenth and the seventeenth century permanent theatre buildings appeared, with Shakespeare's famous Globe theatre first constructed in 1598.

Theatre in a Colder Clime

The first purpose built theatres in a thousand years were open air theatre spaces where performances took place in the day time. Audiences crowded around a high thrust stage as they had in earlier days, when theatre was performed in the market place or inn courtyard, and the more expensive seats were under cover in tiers around the walls of the theatre. Shakespeare still works well today as a theatre form in the open air.

However, companies still had to tour to make ends meet and formal theatres were few and far between, so actors were forced to continue with the rigours of the market place and the portable stage. Whilst permanent theatre buildings proliferated, street and pub theatre lived on until the nineteenth century.

Within the theatres the atmosphere was totally controlled and the design of the theatre space evolved to the way we know it today. The replacement of chandeliers with gas lighting in the early nineteenth century, followed by limelight and in the 1880s, electricity, enabled larger theatres to be built and spectacular sceneic effects and huge crowd scenes created and the auditorium lights to be dimmed for the first time, finally dividing the audience completely from the actors on stage and preparing the way for the cinema.

Theatre Starts to Die

By the middle of the twentieth century some of the functions of theatre transformed themselves into film and television and theatre audiences had by the 1930s dropped to alarmingly low levels. Living theatre, a form of human communication that had lasted for tens of thousands of years, diminished in most people's lives.

Theatre had long since left the streets and the village green and its role as an integrated part of the community's life. It had become a formal and largely middle-class activity to be paid for and watched in a prescribed space. As drama had retreated from its religious origins a greater reliance was placed on technique. Actors are trained to excel in these spaces far from the community in which they live. They use texts drawn from cultures often far removed from their own. Because theatre had lost its mass appeal, the costs were not supported by the size of the audiences. Government grants were given to keep the art form alive. The audience became specialist and was firmly placed in the role of consumer and not invited to join in the process. The cost of tickets even in a subsidised form was relatively expensive and theatre became an activity to be enjoyed only by the few. Live theatre had all but vanished from the lives of the majority of people.

It is essential that human beings do not hand their creativity over to others and become mere consumers of culture but remain a vital part of a living arts world. Theatre is an important form of self-expression for all of us, but to allow it to thrive it must return to the community. It must leave its preconceptions behind and

join the world in which it lives. Theatre is not a
building, it is a human activity to be shared by all. Here
is a poem by Brecht which captures this idea.

You artists who perform plays
In great houses under electric suns
Before the hushed crowd, pay a visit some time
To that theatre of the street.
The everyday, thousandfold, fameless
But vivid, earthly theatre fed by the daily human
     contact
Which takes place in the street.
Here a woman from next door imitates her landlord:
Demonstrating his flood of talk she makes it clear
How he tried to turn the conversation
From the burst water pipe. In parks at night
Young fellows show giggling girls
The way they resist, and in resisting
Slyly flaunt their breasts. A drunk
Gives us the preacher at his sermon, referring the
     poor
To rich pastures of paradise. How useful
Such theatre is though, serious and funny
And how dignified!

                                    On Everyday Theatre, Bertolt Brecht

Barking Dogs, Crying Children

Reaching the community audience can be difficult. One
leaves the quiet, respectful audience, fingertip lighting
and perfect acoustics and plunges into a random, noisy
and unpredictable situation, reaching audiences
wherever they live, work or congregate, often in the
open air.
   It is difficult to do open air theatre well. It is not as
simple as just taking inside theatre outside and hoping

it will work. The basic form is different and the techniques involve a different discipline and hard work. Some street sellers perform wonderfully to their potential buyers. I once watched a salesman in Darwin go through a routine from which an actor could learn a great deal. He set up a small table and at once called the crowd to gather round. His hands dug deep into a chest of jewels and pearls which evoked in us feelings of our long lost fantasies of finding hidden treasure. He flattered the women in the audience and insulted, in a playful way, some of the men. He was a shrewd judge of human nature and his innuendoes and double meanings were on the edge but never alienated the audience. His patter never faltered. He looked you in the eye and invited intimacy and friendship. He was so pleasant and like the crowd so much, he said, that he had decided to give away not just one, not just two, but three gold rings to the first person to put ten dollars in his hands. A woman in the front row leapt forward and slapped ten dollars on the table. She was delighted with her good fortune. The trade continued over the next forty minutes at a steady rate which must have turned over hundreds of dollars. He was so exhausted at giving away his wares that he called a halt and the crowd dispersed. The woman who had received the three gold rings turned up to help him clear up. She was, of course, a plant in the audience. He moved off to his next performance.

That scene reminded me too of the traders of India and Morocco where allure is used to arrest your attention. Huge lengths of silks are unrolled by throwing them in the air, fruit is sold by pressing a delicious sample in your mouth, chairs and tea suddenly appear as if by magic for your convenience as a dazzling display of goods passes by your eyes. Musical instruments are played or clothes modelled by a seemingly endless group of staff. You are involved in a carefully orchestrated piece of theatre before you know it and of course the price must be paid by purchasing something.

Rubbing Elbows

While the aims of the theatre worker are different, the techniques are not. The object is to attract the audience and enthral them in spite of themselves; to arouse their curiosity and keep their expectations in suspense as the theatre unfolds before their eyes. There is no box office, no backstage, no program and no curtain. An audience in the street will simply walk away if it does not relate to the theatre being presented.

Here is what Peter Shuman of the legendary 'Bread and Puppet Theatre' said about his work:

> A theatre is good when it makes sense to people. We have had our best—and sometimes our most stupid—performances in the streets. It stops people in their tracks to see those large puppets, to see something theatrically outside theatre. They can't take the attitude that they've paid money to go into a theatre to "see something." Suddenly there is this thing in front of them, confronting them ... You don't make a point unless a five year old girl can understand it. If she gets it the grown ups will too. The show almost has to be stupid. It has to be tremendously concentrated. You need that intensity in the street much more than in a theatre. Indoors you get by with technique, by sticking to your dialogue, but on the streets you come across only if you have your mind on WHAT HAS TO BE DONE. The space we reject is traditional theatre—it is too comfortable, too well known. Its traditions upset us,

people are numbed by sitting in the same chairs in the same way. It conditions their reactions. But when you use the space you happen to be in you use it all, the stairs, the windows, the streets, the doors. We'll do any play anywhere—provided we can fit the puppets in ... Some of our shows are good and some are bad, but all of our shows are for good against evil.

New Directions, Peter Burton and John Lane

TWO

■

Some Methods of Communication

To keep an audience and communicate with them I have seen four methods used to good effect and although these do not exhaust the different forms it helps to bring the most successful into focus.

METHOD 1 — THE STORY

Telling Stories

The simple act of relating an experience to others for information, education, amusement and reflection on the human condition—what will happen next? Will the evil forces triumph? Will the lovers be united? Can the baby be saved in time? Who can bring justice? One of the great driving forces in the human makeup is curiosity and the story as a form uses this force to good effect. It has a beginning, a middle and an end and because of this the theatre form must be specific. The power of the piece is dependent on the audience seeing the entire show and therefore the length of the show is dependent on the time the audience can watch.

For example if the troupe are putting on a show to commuters there is little point in doing a half hour drama. Conversely, if the show is performed to an audience who have gathered at a festival and are comfortably seated on a grassy knoll a five minute show is probably too short. (I say probably because there is another important rule to remember and that is that five minutes of quality is better than a longer period of ill prepared material.)

Let us take the longer show first. The audience must be settled and even know that they will be watching for some time. The length of show can be announced and the company must ensure that the way it's being performed is conducive to a long show. Ron Davis of the great San Francisco Mime Troop, who performed longer style shows on simple stages, gives this advice:

> Select an intimate grassy area in a park or a place where many people congregate, and play on Saturday or Sunday afternoons. Go where the people are—street corners, vacant lots or parks. Set up a portable stage. Set the stage so that the sun is in the face of the actors, not the audience. Begin the show with music, do exercise warm ups, play and sing, parade around the area, attract the audience ... speak out ... Make sure the ground is comfortable and dry for the audience ... Keep the length of the show under an hour and move it swiftly ... Improvise on mistakes ... Use a funny script, adapted for your own purposes ... Cut out excess dialogue ... and clearly delineate the action ... Keep improvising after the show opens. Then it should close better than it began.
>
> *The San Francisco Mime Troupe*, R.G. Davis

The San Francisco Mime Troop became famous as a
radical theatre group in the sixties, not only in what
they put on stage but also because they performed
outside. It was one thing to perform theatre which
criticised the society but quite another to do it in public.
Their social commitment was clear and direct and they
suffered arrest and harassment from police and park
officials. They used a form of traditional Italian theatre
which uses half masks and large gesture (Commedia
dell'arte) and updated it to bring home their views
about the Vietnamese war and other matters. Their
shows were static and used a stage for performance and
the story really worked for them as the audience was
very happy to sit and watch. Their reputation went
before them and the audiences would turn up to see
them and be ready to spend some time enjoying the
show.

Cart Horses and Gypsy Caravans

In 1974 Theatre Workshop, in Edinburgh, wanted to
tour rural villages in Scotland and had put together an
open air show which would be successful without any
prior publicity. The small villages had never seen
theatre of this type in modern times.

The examination of the communities' rhythm was
vital. We timed the show at five o'clock on the village
green each day. This would include the children and
young people home from school and the parents back
from work. It was before tea and the show would go for
about forty minutes which would allow people to have
their evening meal.

It was impossible to rely completely on the story
because some of the audience would only arrive after
the show had begun. We therefore chose a structure that
was an exciting story but was in five clear related parts.

We wanted to allow the village's past to come alive and for the inhabitants to see their medieval environment in a new way, much as their ancestors had, so we chose an 'Everyman' theme. These were some of the oldest plays to be found in the English language and followed the story of a man who meets the devil who tries to steal his soul, a bandit who tries to rob him and various other adventures including the betrayal of a friend and a meeting with death. As actors we were presenting these old shows from a modern perspective.

If we were to present a medieval show, how could we do it while our way of life included fast travel and television and all the very things that the show was trying to compete with? The answer lay, as it so often does, not in the subject matter but in the form. We must travel and live as the old performers did if we were to see the show from their perspective. We chanced on an old wooden gypsy caravan that was a hundred years old but had not changed in style in the past thousand. We made medieval costumes which we wore all the time, cooked over an open fire and we walked between the villages with a carthorse pulling the cart. The first day we put away our twentieth century accoutrements and donned our tights and doublets, harnessed the horse and set off on our journey of sixty miles and twenty shows.

We had a story to tell and we hoped that the audience would be intrigued enough to listen. We set off at a good pace so we would not fall behind the 'schedule' and before an hour was up realised our first mistake—rushing. If we were to perform twice a day and cook and wash our clothes and costumes, look after the horse and remain happy we had to slow down. Our twentieth century rhythm was not suitable for our way of life and the horse who was pulling the three ton load agreed. We must travel at the horse's pace. It was an animal, not a machine.

We arrived at the first village and the whole community came out of their houses to stare. Our friendly greeting was unacknowledged and we were treated with obvious suspicion. We stopped and set up the show. The children stood around and we invited them to sit down. They didn't. They just stared. We called for the village people to come and see the show. They didn't. They just stood far off in small groups.

We started to perform and Death emerged from the grave yard opposite, the Devil from behind the church and a giant on stilts from the ruined castle. Slowly but surely the children got involved and the Everyman characters' problems became theirs. The story had woven its magic. The adults came nearer and by the half way point the show was working. That evening we put on an entertainment in the local pub loosely based on the Chaucer story of the Wife of Bath in which a man tries to find out what pleases women most. It too worked because the relationship of the afternoon had gained the trust we needed.

Both shows invited the audience to join in verbally and contribute their own ideas and humour to the situation. Many of these comments became part of the script and so the whole show became more part of the area.

By the time that we got near the next village on our next day's walk the children were waiting to walk in with us in a grand parade and this time the atmosphere was friendly. The word had got out and the walking was becoming a piece of theatre in its own right.

And so the tour went on with an ever growing excitement in each village we came to. People would bring us food to eat and presents that they felt would help us do the job. All sorts of local people would come and walk with us or join us around the fire at night and exchange stories about their area. Our physical exertion in walking between villages was really appreciated by the community and we, too, were really enjoying the walking. We discovered a great deal about performance and the problems that must have faced the medieval performer. The cart, for example, was heavy and on steep hills ten people were need on ropes to help the horse pull the load up to the top.

Robin Hood

The power of the story also worked well in another situation many years ago where we were asked to produce an open air show for children who were coming to a play program for a whole day. We would have the same children all day and we had to design a show that could sustain a period of four hours.

We used a modern Robin Hood story in which a window cleaner is outlawed by an evil sheriff who tries everything to defeat him. The first part of the story which establishes the plot was static and lasted about forty minutes,. which was the maximum the children would sit however good the show. There were two sub plots: one, the window cleaner's love for his girlfriend and the other Robin's friend's temptation to betray his friendship for money. The children shouted and participated and booed the baddie and encouraged the heroes. The next part of the show involved the kids building a huge environment and helping Robin trick the sheriff and so now everyone was an actor in the play.

At lunchtime there was a break and when we returned we found that Maid Marion was missing. The search was on and the kids and the actors moved into the environment to find the evil sheriff. Theatre had turned into hide and seek. There was a delightful moment when he was spotted. He and his henchman were asleep and Maid Marion was tied up to a tree behind them. A hundred kids crept up, soundlessly stepped over the sleeping Sheriff and freed Maid Marion and, without a sound, escaped. Everyone then made a costume and a disguise and entered the court of King John and the Sheriff to perform an entertainment. This allowed the kids to perform and the actors to sit and watch them. The roles ha been reversed. They all ripped off their disguises and the story ended with justice prevailing.

What was important about that show was that the theatre did sustain four hours and involved the children in many different ways, but it was the story that drove the piece forward.

Shadows on Boats

Short stories can also be effective. We wanted to put on a small shadow puppet play where the audience could see the shadows of the puppets on the screen lit at the back by a flame. But the screen was on a boat moving past an audience on a river at night at a slow walking pace. The puppets themselves needed a story to make them relevant and therefore a story was enacted that was only three minutes long. The audience would be able to see the whole show even though it was passing by. The story, believe it or not, was about the rise and fall of modern society. A person grew a flower and then a tree. The tree turned into a highrise and then the person was trapped by evergrowing buildings which turned into silos holding rockets. The person destroyed the rockets and the flowers grew again. A lovely tale told in three minutes.

Choose Carefully

But things can go wrong. At the Edinburgh Festival Fringe I worked on an open air show about John McLean who, in the early part of the century was harassed and gaoled for his communist leanings. His trial was a farce and we decided to re-enact the story. But I made a number of decisions that were doomed to failure. The tense drama of the courtroom, so suited to inside theatre, vanished when produced outside and the weather and wind completely destroyed the atmosphere. This was matched with the fact that the actors, who were young people from a large housing scheme in Glasgow, were being asked to perform in a show of which they had no real understanding. The position of the show was on a hill which, although spectacular, was very windy and blew the large visual images down. It was a disaster: the wrong show for the wrong space with the wrong people. I would have been better starting with the young people's ideas and choosing the space and form that suited them, but I had tried to impose the theatre on the situation instead of the other way round and paid the price.

METHOD 2 — THE VISUAL EVENT

Natural Theatre of Bath

The next method does not involve a story in any way. It is the type of theatre that creates an event. It is an excellent form for situations in which an audience is coming and going and can watch the whole thing or just catch a small section. One of the great groups that I have watched working in this way is the Natural

Theatre of Bath in England. They dress as characters and set up situations. For example they turn up as people riding ostriches which presents an illusion that the actor is riding on the bird. On the surface the actors are trying to control the anarchistic birds that run riot in the crowds, but of course controlling the entire effect. It disrupts the norm, creates anarchy and the audience are at once involved.

This type of theatre is very difficult to do well and communication between the members of the group must be excellent. Each member must be an expert in making good theatre happen and the group tuned to exploit the moment. But in some ways it is the purest form of street theatre because it depends on the audience entirely and the theatre that is created involves them in every way. The actor and audience become one in a celebration of the moment which is by its very nature real.

The Natural Theatre also turns up as security men in reflector sunglasses to examine the place for security for a fictional visit by the Queen, or as civil defence workers to stage a practice session in what to do when faced with a nuclear bomb blast. Their theatre can happen anywhere for any amount of time. Yet their themes have real significance and bring into focus vital questions about the way we live our lives.

This type of theatre is very exciting to perform. Each moment is new and challenging and when a good experienced team is working well, it is very close to being totally integrated with its audience.

Almost all theatre is built on a base of pretence. The actors pretend to be someone else and although it might seem spontaneous it is well rehearsed with every move planned. Even improvised theatre has rules which the actors follow. 'Situation' theatre can get to the sublime state of not knowing what is going to happen next, yet the theatre is not lost and the group keeps producing dynamic illusions, often with the help of the audience. Peter Brook has written:

> Putting over something in rough conditions is like a revolution, for anything that comes to hand becomes a weapon. Rough theatre does not pick and choose. It is not trying to present a finished product. It is not asking the audience to judge the theatre but be part of it. (It) does not want the audience to take stock of the actor's talent because that takes away from the reality of the place.

The Essendon Policewomen's Band

This show was conceived in Scotland at a festival when a band was inviting people to dance. The general public started to join in and the music was going full tilt when a policewoman who was on duty and had been watching suddenly joined the dancers. There was a stunned silence and then a great cheer as she took the floor. The effect on the crowd was electrifying and the whole dance floor was swept with a feeling of joy because music had swept away even the reserve of the police.

In Melbourne I worked with West Theatre on the idea until it grew into a full marching band of actors and musicians dressed as policewomen. There have been as many as twelve in the band with the different characters being played by both men and women, usually in equal numbers. They march and play music but it is not in any way military. They explode into the streets with driving South American rhythms using complex drumming, saxophones and trumpet.

I remember one show in Carlton in Melbourne when the eggs we used in a juggling act had been forgotten. Missing props could spread panic in actors locked into the concept of finished, preconceived theatre. The show stopped and the hunt for six eggs was on. The audience searched their handbags and their groceries and the policewomen were in nearby shops and asking the drivers of a line of cars to help. Suddenly from one of the shops a shopkeeper ran up to the crowd with his hand raised in triumph. 'I got the eggs!' he cried and the crowd cheered and the show went on. In such cases the actor and audience are integrated. Nothing can go wrong because there is no tension to 'present' theatre—only the joyful interaction between actor and audience. As John Fox, from Welfare State International Theatre Company, says: 'We have no cultural product for sale.'

Sometimes people reject the product whether it's for sale or not. We presented a Policewomen show in a pub in Portland in Victoria and at one point a dock worker got up and punched me on the jaw!

The Policewomen also have a show to present which is a mixture of music, songs and circus skills which can be presented for five minutes of half an hour depending on the situation. The presentation of skills is very important. The line between a shambles and excellent instant theatre is a fine one and skill plays a real part in the process. If the audience see a crazy group of people just mucking about they feel they are being used, but if the group displays skill the audience feel they are being offered something and respond warmly.

This sort of theatre has two main aims. The first is to fully integrate the theatrical form into the modern street environment. The second is to produce an image and a dynamic which brings to the surface feelings that are usually kept firmly under wraps.

One of the most extraordinary shows that the Policewomen did was in north-west Australia to an Aboriginal group at the local park in Kununurra.

We were there to perform to the local people but took the opportunity to plan an extra show for Aboriginal people. We were taken to the 'town camp' where the authorities had built breeze block houses and rude shelter for washing and toilets and the like. At eight o'clock the community worker put up a single spot light and that was it.

We changed into our policewomen costumes and marched, playing South American rhythms, into the spot light. There were about forty Aboriginal people. We started our show and the reaction was amazing. The children were literally helpless with laughter and the adults not far behind. The natural warmth of the response was wonderful.

After we had finished we were led to the front of the audience and sat down as official guests. For the next half hour we watched a stunning display of their own dances and it was a privilege to see the dancing of a culture that had remained intact for forty thousand years. We had exchanged cultural events at a level that shared the same form if not the same spirituality and had a chance to communicate on a unique level which transcended our differences.

METHOD 3 — THE VISION

Modern Shamans

The third form of street theatre that can be used is mystery. These shows are produced to conjure up magical, beautiful, horrific and mysterious images. There are many excellent groups that do this including Odin Teatret from Denmark, Dogg Troep and Trajekt Theatre from Holland and La Burbuja Teatro and Semola in

Spain. These shows do not usually invite participation but provide powerful images for the audience to relate to. It is their very isolation from the norm that makes them powerful and the audience is forced to think and interpret the images they see before them. It can of course be rejected by the audience as too esoteric and the skill in bringing together the mysterious and the ordinary has to be high.

Engineers of the Imagination

There is no finer group at doing this than Welfare State International Theatre Company in England who have been working for many years with images in open air situations. They are a group of visual artists and musicians who present mysterious theatre but have never felt that the mystery is above the understanding of the community. In fact their policy is to take theatre everywhere that people gather and perform for them. Their theatre is important because they reject the notion that only the educated middle class are able to interpret the esoteric. Their work is a beautiful blend of visual images, music and song which appeals to anyone watching and yet allows the audience to interpret for themselves. There is no right or wrong interpretation of the piece but as many ways of looking at it as there are people in the audience.

The first I saw of their work was a show in a small seaside town in Scotland. Their costumes were the strangest combination of rubbish, personal objects and oddments. They wove music, puppets, extraordinary visual images and strange songs into a series of scenes which continued to amaze the crowd and myself. There was no story that we could see but the show conveyed feelings in a dream-like form that the audience could not fail to be involved with.

The form can certainly show struggle and violence, but also the emotional world with hope and longing, humour and celebration, and most of all dreams, presented in a sensual way with dance, music, energy and colour.

The piece must dance and move, making statements through clear images. There can be jokes, oratory, dialogue, song, rhetoric if necessary. Rhythm and posture, colour and texture speak volumes when employed with care and imagination.

Above all, enjoy it, be proud of your performance and open up to the audience—that communicates most of all.

Sue Fox,
Engineers of the Imagination, Coult and Kershaw

Chrome

An Australian group—Chrome—directed by Tony Strachan is another example of mystery in the streets; but how different they are from the ragged and anarchistic figures of Welfare State. Three actors dress immaculately in strange costumes, they wear reflector sunglasses and have combed their hair back slick on their heads. They move through the streets playing bits of strange music and singing pieces of songs. Their movement is slow and can almost be seen as dance. They stop in front of an audience and perform a mysterious show whose meaning is obscure. They cut out their audience and do not communicate with anyone but themselves. What does it mean? what are they doing? Where are they from? The questions are intriguing and the answers within yourself.

Stalker stilt walking theatre group from Sydney have an international reputation not only for the sheer skill of their stilt walkers but also the images they produce.

They have taken our childhood memories of circus stilt walkers and turned them into visions of wildly moving dancers in exotic costumes mixed with strange images, music and sounds and in doing so have awakened our dreams.

I believe that good open air theatre should never have to explain what it is about: the form of the show is the message. Theatre should never involve the turgid use of symbols for symbol's sake.

In 1975 I went to visit Peter Shuman at Bread and Puppet Theatre in the U.S.A. The group had left the cities to live in rural Vermont, several hours drive from Boston. They live within the same area and when they don't produce theatre they farm maple syrup. I was invited to stay the night and I asked Peter to tell me about his work.

He stood up and said that he could do better than that, he could show me. We walked out to a very large New England barn and along each wall were laid out various sections. In each section were the puppets and images from many shows the group had done. The visual impact was extraordinary. Each show through the years was in a different set of colours and each exhibition told its own story. The puppets were wonderful, ranging in size from tiny three inch figures to sixteen foot giants. Along side the puppets were masks of real beauty and other images and props used for the show.

I recognised the images which had become famous in the Washington moratoriums against the Vietnam war. There was a huge pterodactyl which was shaped like a B-52 bomber which took many people to work it, and dozens of white masks. I remembered the huge animal bomber being carried past the Washington Memorial in a mass rally with several dozen actors with the white death masks on it. It had a huge impact for the tens of

thousands of people protesting who every night
watched the media show the real B-52s dropping
napalm. Receiving our perceptions of the world through
television moves us one step away from the experience
but theatre has the power to bring us face to face with
reality again.

Dartington

David Harding, Scotland's well known town artist, was
teaching at Dartington College in England and asked
myself and another artist, Ken Wolverton, to help with
an open air show. The performance included all the
students and staff. The college felt that it was vital to
bring all the different departments of the arts together
for cross disciplinary projects at least once a year. They
planned to hold a Spring Festival in the nearby town of
Totnes in Devon. The show had an interesting form
which took the audience of several hundred through the
village to watch various theatre pieces in suitable
surroundings. The performance represented the
vanquishing of winter and the victory of spring. The
show was all ready to go with large visual images to
represent the two seasons.

Ken and I decided that we would move through the
audience as the spirit of winter, neutrally observing our
own death. We dressed in beautiful grey suits, white
gloves and white death make-up and moved into the
crowd at the beginning of the show. We moved in very
slow motion to convey the feeling of death and moved
along with the crowds watching the show. At first the
audience around us laughed and expected us to smile
but, keeping to one of the cardinal rules of street theatre
which is to never break character, we remained 'dead.'
The good humour gave way to resentment and even
anger as individuals asked us to respond. Every part of

me wanted to break out and entertain but I kept silent. As the show continued people moved away and discussed what we were meant to be. Ken and I acted in concert and were moving as a team when a clown, who was to move through the audience playing pipes, danced up. Without prompting we very slowly lifted our arms and pointed at him.

I suddenly felt the electricity flow and the moment became astounding. It was as if death had warned him that his time would come. He fell back as if poleaxed and ran off. The actor, a young man called Paul Yeoman, realised the power of what had happened and returned throughout the afternoon to challenge us. The performance was, after an hour and a half, an act of stamina but the longer we maintained the mood the more strength it gained.

METHOD 4 — SKILLS

Pianos on Chins

The fourth type of successful open air theatre is the display of skill. This is often seen in the streets of western society as buskers play music or jugglers entertain. But I have often seen these simple and age old entertainments really work as theatre. Jugglers throw clubs to one another, fire-eaters swallow flames, stiltwalkers play music in beautiful costumes, a single violinist plays on a street corner; all contribute to the experience of art and the people. Most are busking and asking the audience to throw money into a hat, but there is now a section in many arts budgets where funds are allocated to allow these entertainments to go on. The organisers are now realising that our streets have become sterile wastelands where colour and life have gone. Our city landscapes are devoted to the selling of products and the passage of cars. As a place for people our inner cities are dying. How good it is to see the sterility broken up by live performance of music, theatre and comedy.

Some artists have taken these skills to great heights. I have seen cellos balanced on noses, pianos spun on feet, wonderful clowns performing *Macbeth,* excellent acrobats performing impossible acts, escape artists dangling at fifty feet, and magicians of great cunning thrilling the crowds. I have heard music by individuals, bands and orchestras as well as the wonderful bicycle band in Melbourne which is a seven piece brass band all on one enormous bike! I have seen puppets both big and small bring the city landscape to life and heard poets and writers tell us about their worlds. The list is endless. How much poorer the world would be without them and how much richer it would be with many more.

PART TWO

■

Community Theatre

Professional theatre makers
and community working together

THREE

■

Involving the Community

The world, I think, is moving towards unity, a unity won not alone by the necessities of the physical developments themselves, but the painful and confused re-assertion of man's inherited will to survive. When the peace is made, and it will be made, the question Greece asked will once again be asked ... by the man who can live out his life without fear of hunger, joblessness, disease ... where are we going now we are together? For, like every act man commits, the drama is a struggle against his own mortality, and meaning is the ultimate reward for having lived.

ARTHUR MILLER
The Book of Theatre Quotes, Gordon Snell

The building of a piece of theatre in the community can be likened to building a house and the work of the director can be seen in the same light as that of an architect. Both the architect and the director receive a budget and ideas about what people want and they then design a 'blueprint' consulting the client at each step of the way, keeping as closely to the 'brief' as possible. They get together a group of 'builders' who are best suited to the particular project and then put the whole project together. They then present the finished plan to the clients and make changes if they are not happy and when everyone is satisfied then the project moves forward.

The building of a piece of theatre can be used as a tool for expression by any community of people. The word 'community' describes almost any section of society that is gathered together and can be defined by work, geographical location, common interest, ethnic origin or a living situation. It implies a state of 'communion' or fellowship, concord, agreement and even a state of unity. However, most 'communities' are not harmonious units of common purpose but an amalgam of different groups and individuals struggling with a common identity. Each community has its own special dynamics and character and each piece of theatre must be designed to meet those individual needs.

I always take a deep breath as I enter a new community as an explorer might in seeing a new country ahead. A whole culture lies undiscovered. As well as exciting possibilities, there are dangers and pitfalls waiting to trap the innocent. There is also a great responsibility in interaction with a specialised community, as careless and insensitive work can severely damage the very culture that one is trying to enhance. The work of cultural expression can be made more complex when the community in which one works is in social difficulty, and yet it is in those very communities that the work is often needed most. Working class ghettos, ethnic minorities, difficult work places and dozens of other situations all warrant theatre

9 months	Week 7	Week 6	Week 5	Week 4	Week 3	Week 2	Week 1	SHOW	Show + 1 week
Plan, research, design and fund the project	Blueprint done in detail							S	Bump Out
		workshops and rehearsals						H	Return equipment
				props and costumes				O	
				staging			rig stage	W	Feedback
									Obtain record
				plan sound			rig sound		Reports + accounts
				plan lights			rig lights		Social gathering
			ongoing budget						
	plan box office/publicity/insurance/transport/contracts/accomodation etc								
	Consult with community and arts team throughout								Assessment

EXAMPLE 1: NOTIONAL TIME PLAN FOR PROJECT

at its most dynamic, yet they are all potentially explosive if not handled with the greatest care. The process of building a show must not be rushed, especially at the development stage. If there are applications to be submitted then they can take up to a year to process and usually nothing can happen without proper funding. Some projects can move more quickly if finance is already in place, but it is always best to develop a good workable plan rather than rush into a project unprepared. I have included a time plan for a recent project which might be useful. (See Example 1)

A community might invite theatre workers to come into their community but may not be aware of what is likely to happen. This 'invitation' is a delicate business because the person or group of people doing the inviting might not in any way represent the community. This has often happened when well meaning funders or local politicians feel that a 'show' will be just the thing to help a particular community, when there has been no local discussion or consultation. The theatre workers arrive and find that nobody knows anything about it. I have found that most communities want to participate in positive action but resent deeply not being consulted as to its form. So where does one go to find the 'community' to ask its opinion?

Approaches differ but I have found that the public meeting is not an effective way of canvassing local views for an arts project, however, I hasten to add, some have found it effective. I prefer approaching more informally. People in any community gather in groups and it is a case of finding the ones that local leaders participate in. One must look for the people of action in any group—the people who get out and 'do it' rather than talk about it. But one rule of thumb is that it is important not to just take the surface view, but to dig deeper to find out where the real representatives of the people lie. The situation is rarely what it first seems. This is the most important part of any project, because if this first stage is not done properly the whole project starts off on the wrong foot and sometimes can never be salvaged.

I find that I can generally identify about five sections in a community that one can look to for support.

One first group to contact could be the local politicians. They can be of great help in securing funding or helping release government resources but they are usually not involved in the day to day running of a community. However, it is a very good idea to visit the local politicians and discuss the overview of the project and measure their enthusiasm for the general idea. One can meet some great people who have given their 'all' to the community in which they live and who have given the arts the greatest support. Usually they are happy to help where they can as long as it does not take up too much of their time. Politicians can also be very offended if they are not consulted, however briefly.

The second category could be the local church. They can be of great help and many of the church workers are deeply committed people. They also have invaluable resources and often hold sway over the best spaces in some areas.

The third section of a community might be the school. There are a very large number of teachers in every area: some will live locally. The school is also one of the conduits to the young people of the community and very important in terms of physical resources.

The fourth section is the professional workers. Social workers, for example, are dealing with 'cases' which are the individual problems of the people who come to them. Youth workers and community workers are also useful contacts and already have active networks of local people who might want to participate. Clubs and interest groups as disparate as scouts and parachutists are often run by enthusiastic people who love to join in any project that might see their skills used.

The last and most important group are the natural leaders within the community itself. After all, their commitment that will make or break a project. The local leaders at a grass roots level are not necessarily obvious but they are there to find if one looks. They are the people helping in a practical day to day way. Their support is essential and should be gained before proceeding with any new project.

Any one of the five groups might 'invite' an arts project into the community but before going ahead the invitation should be weighed up against the opinions of the other four.

Why Are You Doing It?

To ask a commitment of a community one must understand one's own reasons for being involved. Saul Alinsky, the father of community development in America and a great model for me, said that the understanding of one's own motives was the most important thing to know about working in the community. No one is purely altruistic in their work with people. We do it because we get something out of it and we must be certain that our exchange with local people is a good one. Are we giving as much as taking? It is a complex question for an arts worker to answer but a vital one to be asked.

My own reason is that I find the artistic challenge of creating theatre with people from all walks of life enormously satisfying. It is a wonderful experience to see theatre come alive in a community and for that community to enjoy and celebrate itself. I love the creation of theatre in unusual spaces with unusual people with all sorts of unusual skills. Theatre is as magical as the human imagination will let it be and when one sees its magic working with ordinary people one can see its vital importance to our society and to the individual in that society.

Examination of Resources

Every community has different physical resources. Rehearsals might be in the back rooms of pubs, old factories, barns, front rooms, offices, storerooms, empty restaurants, churches. I have even been put in a mortuary, which I hasten to add was unused at the time. Space can always be found if the community is behind you.

The local area also has material resources in its local factories, shops, warehouses and businesses and few people mind helping if projects are carefully explained.

Money is always hard to get from local authorities but with good will they can help with transport, premises, trucks, tools and dozens of other sundry items needed for theatre. Two words of caution. The first is to make sure it is free or the price of help has been discussed *in writing*. Local councils can be very helpful until you find that they are charging you for all their work. It is important to put your requirements and receive your response *in writing* when dealing with government. Nine times out of ten a reasonable request will meet with help if pursued with energy and optimism.

The Community Voice

By far the best resource in any community is the talent and enthusiasm of the people, the human resource. Sometimes these talents are waiting to be discovered, but they are always there. Musicians, actors, dancers, visual artists in every shape and form can be found, especially in the young. Even activities that seem a long way distant from the arts can be wonderful if utilised in the right way. Rock climbers, electricians, archers, gym clubs, weight lifters are only some of the groups who have helped us in projects.

The most difficult job is to identify the person who can somehow sum up what the community really feels; the community's voice. Through this person – and there is always someone filling this role in a community, one can find the true spirit of community.

Getting the Feeling

While the resources are being discovered there is a parallel process taking place and that is research. This involves finding out about the area's internal beat and rhythm. How has its history affected the present life of the community? What are people's fears? What would they like to see happen? Where do the tensions lie? How do people live? What are their symbols? What do different age groups think? The answers themselves are sometimes not as important as the way people answer.

Now one has a rough 'feeling' for the community as a guide and has consulted the leaders and the local people. Now comes the most delicate part of the theatre process—the construction of the project.

Community Development

The homework must be done thoroughly and the community must be behind the project but there comes the time to make decisions based on what has been found. This decision-making process varies from project to project but there is an important factor to consider *before* taking on any arts project in a community. As outsiders to an area one must see all projects in terms of the value that the piece of theatre can give. If there is an existing network of community activists, how can the theatre further their work and, if there is not, how can a cultural event help focus one? If this is the first theatre event staged in the area how can the momentum be carried on after the project is finished? If there have been previous shows how can this one develop the theatre's quality and improve the artistic decision making? All these questions are tied up with defining clear aims for the project in the light of past work, the present situation and future development. What does the community want in the long term as well as in the short term?

Decision Making

The project in a community belongs to that community and it is essential for the local group to decide what it wants from a cultural event. Yet the problem often emerges that people do not know how to make a decision about a theatre project when they do not have the experience and knowledge behind them. In fact, that is why they have organised the outsiders to help them. It is totally irresponsible of outside arts workers to come in to a community and demand that the local people make all the decisions in the name of democracy, if those local people do not have the confidence and experience to succeed. This sort of attitude is as bad as allowing local people no access to the decisions.

The most important point in all this is that the outside art workers and the community must come to agreement about what decisions are to be made by whom and who carries what responsibility before the project starts. Then it is written down ... it becomes a sort of artistic agreement.

It is a question of the artist and the community learning about each other. Some have said that it is the theatre workers' job to teach the community to take over their function and for that community to have the ability to create theatre unaided. This point of view demeans both the artist and the community. The theatre maker has spent years learning the trade and a community can no more learn those skills in the length of a project than the artist can learn how to be an electrician, a carpenter or a doctor in a few weeks. The artist has specialist skills which can be used by a community to great effect and it is a question of educating both sides to the ways in which this is to be done.

There is a key way in which the community can keep control over the project and that is for them to raise and control the budget. A group of people have no real control over anything if they are not holding the purse strings. This financial control gives the local people the right to spend their cultural money as they see fit. They apply to the arts funders and in doing so begin to exercise their rights to arts money. After the project is over they can also evaluate the good the project did the community and weigh its value against other priorities. It is a triumph for the arts that in spite of other pressing needs the community often sees the real value in cultural development and puts it high on their action list again and again.

But there are hidden problems in a community holding the finances which can be very dangerous to the project. When the project is designed and the budget agreed then the theatre show can go ahead, but if the community refuse to spend the money as planned or conversely remain inflexible in the way the money is allocated in spite of changing circumstances, then the whole production will be at risk.

The professional should be well versed in running a budget and should be trusted to do so. The amount of production money should be clearly outlined at the beginning of the project and given to the arts team to spend. If major changes are needed then the artists and the community can draw up a new budget and take it from there.

Communities Beware

Communities that are thinking of employing professional artists in a project should take a good deal of care in selecting who they should engage. The first step is to selct the type of artist one needs. Almost all theatre workers are specialists, therefore it is important to select an artist who is experienced in the area the community wants to explore.

Once the community have found artists who work in the field they want to explore, then it is vital to examine the competence of the artists involve. Videos and photographs of past projects, talk to the organisers from as many other past projects as possible, references are very helpful and newspaper and other reports of their work can be consulted.

Often it is a good idea to find a director before selecting other members of an arts team. A good experienced arts director will be able to help a community select the right professional arts staff for its needs.

Advice

If one is embarking on a project for the first time it is important to get good advice and sometimes this is difficult to find. One might contact a theatre group which has been doing this work for many years such as Brisbane's excellent Streets Arts or Albury Wodonga's Murray River Performing Group. Other similar groups can be found in different centres and can be found through the local Office of the Arts. The Australia Council have officials in each department who will do their best to assist enquiries and they have an excellent library of past projects. Many areas have their own Community Arts Officers and can be contacted through the local Council and most States have community Arts Networks which might be helpful. Local Arts Councils in rural areas might be able to give advice as well as resources for projects.

FOUR

■

Planning
the Event

You know, I wouldn't go out to Greenland and perform for the Eskimos and do Mozart operas, because I don't think they have heard one—but if I were to go out in a kayak and turn upside down and stay under water for ten minutes, I think they would die laughing.

VICTOR BORGE
The Book of Theatre Quotes, Gordon Snell

Planning the Event

The first and most critical decision to be taken is what form the theatre will take, for it is from this that the rest follows. To arrive at the form one must weigh up the aims of the project, the aspirations of the community, the budget, the talents and resources available, the poetic landscape and context.

Sometimes the community have a firm idea for a story they want to tell or something they want to communicate which gives the artist a foundation to work on. At other times the ideas have to be built up from scratch. But whatever the starting point, certain key decisions have to be made.

Inside\Outside

The show could be performed inside or outside. Each setting has its own advangtages and disadvantages. An inside show has a controlled space and is very secure. It allows scripts to develop and the show can be marketed with a ticket price. Outside shows can produce a great deal of excitement and interest in the community because the show is right there in their midst, but equipment is at risk and it can be difficult to control box office. These are two completely different ways of approaching theatre and with two very different social and theatrical results. Even the teams needed to produce them might be very different.

But the effort to set up in an outside space can be well worth it. In October 1991 we produced *Macbeth* in the Katherine Gorge in the Northern Territory. Here was an awe inspiring space which was over 150 million years old. The production difficulties were immense as the space lay on Aboriginal land with a twenty-five minute boat ride to reach it. Boats had to bring in everything for the production and that included a half ton generator for the lights. The cast of sixty had to be shipped in for their rehearsal and Macbeth and Lady Macbeth had their own boat. The audience had to make the trip in large ferries each night, navigating in the darkness. But it was all worth the effort for the privilege of performing in such a beautiful and powerful place. It was a show to remember for the rest of one's life.

Size of the Show

The size of the show is important and a great
determining factor. With a small group of actors one can
develop a highly concentrated performance and with a
cast of a hundred and one can deliver a spectacular.
Both have their strengths but the choice must be made
carefully.

Number of Performances

Certain shows work well if they are designed to run for
a specified number of performances. These might have a
small cast and be relatively simple to produce from a
technical point of view. In other cases a one off
theatrical event produces a better result because all of
one's resources can be concentrated into a single night.
One might think that it is a waste to run a whole project
for just one night, but a single event can reach a very
large number of people if it is constructed to do so:
more people in fact than a run of many nights.

Kind of Audience

It is vital to think about the potential audience. It makes
a huge difference to the product. The show might be
designed for the local community in which it is based or
for the wider community. It might be going on tour or
taken into a special situation. All these factors are vital
in the form the show takes and it does not matter how
good a show is, if it is being taken to the wrong
audience.

All these are critical decisions in achieving a successful
result and must be decided before the show is finally
constructed. But whatever type of show is chosen it is

Shadow puppets. *(Photo: Neil Cameron. Image: John Bolton)*

Two winter figures, Dartington College, England, 1979. *(Photo David Harding)*

LEFT: Whangarei Show, 1982, New Zealand. *(Photo: Northern Advocate New Zealand)*

ABOVE: Priesthill Glasgow, 1980, music rehearsal. *(Photo: Neil Cameron)*

BELOW: Senior citizens' choir, Whangarei All Human Circus, New Zealand, 1982.

LEFT: Essendon Policewomen's Marching Band, WEST Theatre, Melbourne. (*Photo: Performers Management*)

BELOW: The buffalo, emblem of the Philipinnes for the Arafura Games, Darwin, 1991. (*Makers: Francis Corby, Phyllis Aquilina. Photo: Jude Swift*)

Death Ship, Seagrass Event III – the saving of the wetlands, Hastings, 1990. *(Image: Neil Cameron. Photo: Ponch Hawkes)*

RIGHT: 'Fire on the Water', Mindil
Beach, Darwin, 1988.
(Photo: N.T News)

LEFT: 'Macbeth' in the Katherine
Gorge (Nitmiluk) 1991.
(Photo: N.T News)

Witches, 'Macbeth' in the Katherine Gorge, 1991. *(Photo: Andrew Cruse)*

The cast, 'Macbeth' in the Katherine Gorge, 1991. *(Photo: Andrew Cruse)*

Mother puppet, May Day parade, Darwin, 1989. *(Image: Neil Cameron, Tim Newth)*

Frill-necked lizard, built with the help of school students for the Pacific School Games, Darwin. *(Image: Tim Newth)*

People from Darwin's ethnic communities prepare for the Arafura Games Opening Ceremony,1991. *(Photo: Jude Swift)*

vital that it is costed properly and accurately budgeted. Certain types of shows are much more economical than others and the amount of money one has to spend has a great bearing on the final decision.

Pieces of a Puzzle

Each theatre worker has individual methods in building up a show and much depends on their own vision and experience. I work from a plan which is almost like a mathematical puzzle. The community and the theatre team have decided the way the show will be performed, the research has been done, the resources have been investigated and the aim of the project carefully worked out. I lay out all these facts and then construct the show using the following factors: The space, the content, the music and auxiliary arts, recruitment and casting, artistic team, writer, technical crew, the budget and the resources.

The Budget

The blueprint of the show has been constructed and now the budget must be worked out. This is a complex business because it must be based on a realistic fundraising strategy and an accurate costing of the show that is being planned.

Let us take the fundraising strategy first. As mentioned elsewhere, the raising of funds has to be done well in advance of the project and some government bodies can take many months to deliver a decision. It can then take up to three further months to crank up the project from that point. In other words, one can be looking at a year's delay between conceiving the project and starting work. As a rough guide I have drawn up a chart to

SOURCE	NOTIONAL TIME SCALE
PHILANTHROPIC TRUSTS	Check library for book on Philanthropic Trusts
ARTS COUNCILS	Varies. See local branch for details
FUND RAISING SCHEMES	Held in advance
FESTIVALS/EVENTS	1 Year if possible
CORPORATE FUNDING	9 Months
FEDERAL GOVERNMENT PROGRAMS	9 Months
AUSTRALIA COUNCIL	6/9 Months. Write for details
STATE GOVERNMENT DEPARTMENTS	6/9 Months
LOCAL GOVERNMENT FUNDS	4 Months
LOCAL GOVERNMENT *IN KIND* SUPPORT	2 Months
IN KIND SUPPORT FROM BUSINESS	A few weeks
BOX OFFICE	Nights of event
FOOD/DRINK	See on night

EXAMPLE 2: NOTIONAL INCOME SOURCES AND TIME LIMITS

Note: The time limits here are only notional. Check for specific details. Also check closing dates for applications as there can be only one a year.

demonstrate the main sources of funding and the time taken to make applications. (See Example 2)

As shown in the diagram there are many sources of funding and each one demands care and an individual style of approach. The funding criteria for one funding body need not necessarily apply to another. Some projects have many different sources of funds and each of those funding areas might have very different criteria for judging whether a project has gone well. It is vital to present the show one proposes to do in terms that would-be funders understand and to communicate the artistic and social reasons in their terms. Therefore, a careful examination of their funding criteria can be helpful. A philanthropic trust might be interested in funding a theatre piece which it sees as being socially helpful but the Australia Council would be much more interested in the artistic content. It is a question of balance and being able to present the project in the right light.

But before one can raise funds an accurate budget is needed. This can be difficult because in this type of theatre production there are many imponderables. There are the normal theatre items such as costumes, props, publicity and fees, but when there is no ready made environment to perform in and when that environment has to be constructed from scratch then careful planning is needed. Generators, pyrotechnic effects, security, sets, insurance and many other costs associated with this type of show can be expensive and the show must always be tailored financially to realistic expectations of funding.

There is always the question about income at the box office. It is the age-old dilemma of all theatre makers throughout history. How can a show be costed without knowing if people will pay to come and see it? This is where it is vital for communities to hire experienced and

FEES: Director/Writer/Musicians/Artists/Dancers/
Actors/Lighting Crew/Designer/Sound
Technicians/Teachers/Administration Staff/Stage
Manager/Publicity Manager/Other Staff*

WORK SPACE: Rent/Running costs

TRANSPORT: Petrol/Repair/Hire

INSURANCE: Public Liability/Staff/Equipment/Loss of
income (Rain)

LIGHTS: Hire/Breakage (inc. Bulbs)/Scaffolding/ Trees etc

SOUND: Hire/Staging

PUBLICITY: Press/Media ads/Tickets/Poster and
distribution /Handouts/Banners and signs

PROPS AND COSTUMES: Accurate costs

POWER: Generators/Other sources

ADMINISTRATION: Telephone/office/etc/Mail/Fax/
Duplication/Equipment

DONATIONS: St John's Ambulance/Service Clubs, etc

CAR PARK COSTS: Signs/Barricades etc

BOX OFFICE COSTS: Floats etc

AIRFARES AND TRAVEL: Any expenses

PHOTOGRAPHY AND VIDEO: Check all expenses

STAGING: Seats/Stage/Scenery/Scaffolding

MATERIALS: Everything needed

EQUIPMENT AND TOOLS: Everything needed

EXAMPLE 3: NOTIONAL EXPENDITURE BUDGET

*Note: This list is not exhaustive and many items will be added as
each show evolves.*

* *Contracts should be in writing and include all known conditions. They
should contain details of personal insurance and tax arrangements and
include provision for any work needed after the show is over.*

professional teams if they do not want to be left with debts. The show must be designed to attract the size of audience that has been estimated in the budget. I work on a 70% audience attendance in my budget leaving 30% as a leeway. Some theatre producers leave bigger gaps. I have drawn up a fictitious budget based on realistic situations which might be helpful. (See Example 3)

One further point. It is always important to have insurance and to include it is the budget. It in vital to have the public insured through public liability and the staff insured through workcare. But a further type of insurance should be considered if the theatre performance is outside and that is rain cover. The policy will cover loss of earnings due to cancellation because of rain and details can be obtained from a local insurance agent. Insurance of equipment is also worth considering.

THE SPACE

One of the most exciting factors in working outside of the conventional theatre is the selection of a theatre space. The chance to stage theatre in an infinite variety of interesting spaces and the challenge that this presents in a great part of the magic for me. But among a bewildering array of choices the question must be asked: What makes a good theatre space?

There are common factors to all good theatre spaces but it is to be remembered that what is good for one piece of theatre, is not necessarily good for another. If I were to choose one critical factor in a good theatre space it would have to be that the audience and performer are set up in the right relationship for the show one intends to present. In most cases an audience needs to feel comfortable, and anticipatory. The atmosphere is important. Does the production require a feeling of

warmth or of alienation? A feeling of safety or of
disorientation? Is this to be the setting for a large
spectacular or a small, intimate show? Sound is a critical
factor for the good theatre space, as is lighting, and they
must be planned so that everyone in an audience can
hear and see everything clearly. This seems obvious, but
in working in non purpose-built spaces, sound and
lights can be a real problem.

I stand in a prospective space and bring the whole
production to mind. I look at it through the eyes of the
audience member. I go through their experience of
arriving, what they have to eat or drink, where they will
sit and for how long and what they will see and hear. I
come back to the space at the time at which the show
will be held to make sure that the right conditions still
prevail.

Inside Spaces

I have seen all sorts of spaces being used to good effect.
Old buildings such as woolsheds, old houses or even
prisons can all be utilised for their atmosphere and
stamp onto the performance a certain style. Disused
factories or warehouses can be wonderful spaces, as are
all sorts of structures used by modern society. The space
does not even have to be static as was shown by
Theatre Works' excellent production 'Storming Mont
Albert' on a Melbourne tram!

We have sometimes gone to a great deal of trouble to
change a conventional theatre into a new kind of space.
We produced a community show with Maoris and
whites in the North Island of New Zealand. We were
based in an art centre with a modern theatre with a
purpose built stage but that space was 'against' the
feeling of community warmth we wanted to create. We
spent a month building an environment in the art

gallery next door which was a 90 x 90 ft space on the floor with raked seating for five hundred people on three sides. We then put up a circus big top over the space to perform in, with the immediacy of the audience creating an intimate and warm environment. Infinitely preferable to the theatre stage next door.

In South Australia we were to use a large purpose built theatre but instead of asking the audience to sit in the theatre seats we built a cabaret space on the huge stage and closed the curtains. The audience were integrated into the show.

Outside Spaces

The open air gives an enormous amount of atmosphere as one can utilise the setting's natural power and beauty to enhance the performance. The seashore, a forest, the side of a hill, an island, a river and even the urban environment of the modern city can all produce good theatre spaces. Inside spaces built in the open air such as circus tents or marquees can have good atmosphere as well as protection from the weather.

However, it must always be remembered that an open air show brings with it many technical problems such as power, lights, sound, staging and security and all these and many other factors must be costed and taken into consideration before choosing the space.

One must also balance the advantage of the space against the local people's skills and never force them into a space which takes specialist techniques to make it work.

THE CONTENT

There are a number of approaches which might be used for a starting point.

Using History and the Future

The first of these is what I would call a time structure. The show uses the history of the area to bring about an awareness of the present.

An example of this was St. Albans, which is a migrant area in Melbourne, where we produced a show in a circus tent. The area had been developed in the fifties and was steeped in stories of migration from war torn Europe and the struggle of the migrants when they first settled here. The show told this story in the first half and in the second part we looked at the reaction of today's young people to that history.

Another example was in Scotland where a small village had a famous ghost which acted as a catalyst in the show to 'rest' the spirits of the past. It is important to look back into the past, to view the world as it was and to understand the struggles of past generations. 'Time' shows can also move us forward and let us view the future as we might want it or as we might not.

Political Theatre

Another structure is political. It has been the basis and motivation for many community shows where theatre is seen as a vehicle to express a social or political opinion.

Theatre in its very nature needs to transcend the political dialectic if it is to work and yet need not lose any of its bite. Local community shows which are brought about by a feeling of social injustice tend to have local themes which must be handled with extreme sensitivity. It is advisable in some cases to take a real political situation and build around it a 'fiction' which still contains the original feeling.

One example was a show in Liverpool, England where a poor working class community was geographically placed in the middle of a predominantly middle class area. The political representation reflected middle class values and very much victimised the poorer area. The subject matter of the story had to be taken away from this sensitive political situation which would have caused alienation and further problems. The play's plot became a struggle between a fictitious community and a large syndicate who wanted to bulldoze the area for a new holiday and gambling resort. Here we had a 'parallel' situation where the local people needed to save their homes from the blind decisions of outsiders. It expressed the point without causing further division.

A Literary Structure

Another important form is an existing literary structure. In other words to take a 'classic' story and use it as a dramatic vehicle. The whole world of literature is open to a community either as a story or a play.

We were asked to help a community in Glasgow do a show about social injustice. Emile Zola wrote *Germinal* about a French mining village which is eventually brought to its knees by a long strike. However, the cruelty of the mine owners germinates the seed for future struggles for social justice. We updated this plot and transferred the story to Scotland where mines were being closed by the Tory government. It became a moving modern story of a family in Glasgow.

There is the world's selection of plays which include Brecht and Shakespeare which can be used in total or in part and many Australian plays are very suitable to be presented. However, there is much written about this type of production and this book is concentrating on community devised projects.

Topical Subjects

Topical situations can also bring inspiration for plots. We were asked to produce a show for the community of Priesthill in Glasgow which was in severe social decay. The Glasgow Council's answer, as in countless other housing estates, was to knock it down, break up the existing community of extended families and then eventually rebuild another estate, which would in time become another slum, with new tenants.

At that time the Olympics in Russia had just finished with all the bickering about who would participate and who would not. This suggested a plot. The show started with the Olympic committee deciding to stop all this quarrelling about where the Olympics were to be held by putting the alternatives in a hat, and drawing out a name. It turned out to be Priesthill. The Olympic committee wanted to knock it down to build an Olympic village. In the story the local community prevented this and put up the world athletes in their houses. A show with lots of fun but underneath the surface is the real threat of losing their community and how they could fight to save it.

Birth, Love, Death and a Good Laugh

One has always to remember that the issues in a show are not abstract themes developed by a group of theatre professionals in the isolation of the theatre environment, but living issues that affect the individuals who are in the cast and the audience. The greatest care must be taken in the presentation of real issues as the theatre can and does deeply affect people's lives.

All people are interested in the big things of life like birth, love, pain, desire, death, tragedy and humour. It is part of theatre's magic to be able to bring them to life.

Stories of the individual's struggle in the community in which they live can be built up by workshops and discussions with local people.

Sub-plots

The main story is sometimes only part of the 'scenario' which is needed before the show matures as a piece of theatre. One can develop sub-plots which can offer a change of tone or pace or even sometimes help resolve the main plot. These can take the form of love stories, moral dilemmas, characters' personal problems, crimes or conspiracies. In community theatre all these possibilities allow the producer to include facets of the community which are perhaps not suitable for the main plot.

In a production of the *Hunchback of Notre Dame* I was asked by the local festival to include a group of mentally handicapped adults. It was obviously a very sensitive issue in the context of this story. These people found difficulty in learning lines and presenting them in the usual way and yet we felt their inclusion was very important.

We developed a sub-plot where they became a group of town criers who told the story. They did not contribute to the main plot but worked well as a sub-plot moving the story along from scene to scene. But their inclusion in the play gave a new and joyful dimension to the whole.

Beginnings, Middles and Ends

The stories of the world are there for us to use, but it might be good to reflect on a basic principle of the good story in this rhyme:

Aristotle
took another swig from the bottle,
and remarked to a friend:
'A play must have a beginning a middle and an
end.'

Good general advice when devising the story format.
Sometimes the results of foggy plotting can be
disastrous and very frustrating to an audience.

THE STYLE

Much theatre uses a 'naturalistic' form which shows
people talking naturally in a setting which portrays a
scene and we are asked to follow the characters through
the story. This can be effective in community theatre but
really needs a good script and a very controlled space.
  One might choose only one style or the show might
contain a mixture. It is a moveable feast and open to the
skill of the theatre makers, but some suggestions as to
the wide range can be helpful. I believe that it is
important to try to bring in good specialist instructors
where possible, as each of the following forms are crafts
unto themselves.

Inside Styles

Cabaret: An excellent style if you have a small audience
and the show can be in different parts or acts. A good
vehicle for satire and humour but the music must be
good and lively.

Music Hall: Again a style that suits lots of disparate acts
and works well on a proscenium arch stage with
audience participation.

The Musical: A story is mixed with music and dance.

Mime: In spite of its reputation as being silent, this form can be used in all sorts of ways and mixed with dialogue and sound.

Dance: A whole world of excitement and movement from all sorts of cultures and societies. Good and talented teachers can give dance a whole new dimension.

Acrobatics: A good form to be harnessed to a drama where crowd scenes can erupt into action and excitement. Acrobatics can often be linked to circus skills of all kinds. (See 'Circus' in Open air Section.)

The Grotesque: A theatre style of contorted bodies rejected by society, living in an anarchistic world where morals do not match our own.

Melodrama: An overblown Victorian form of theatre which can under certain circumstances be powerful and interesting. Many people parody this type of theatre nowadays but it can have surprising results if it is played with real commitment.

Mask: Commedia del'Arte is a form of Italian half mask with stock characters, but it can be adapted. Full masks of all kinds are powerful and new ways in designing masks can be very exciting.

Puppets: All sorts of puppets from shadows to large scale can be used and transform a scene into magical images.

Ensemble Presentations: This is where the whole group combines to tell a story with few or no props and a maximum use of the body.

Outside Styles

Chorus: A Greek style of group script or song which is very effective in transferring sound in the open air.

Circus: A wonderful array of skills including acrobatics, stilt walking, fire eating, magic, balances, clowning and feats of skill. Good instructors who understand their craft are needed but it is surprising how quickly the young can produce good work.

Large Scale Images: This can include large puppets and effigies, fire sculptures, moving images of all sorts, fireworks and a whole host of special effects.

Mummers and Buskers: The technique of selling a show to an audience from a small stage and through sparkling language and crowd interaction bringing about a show.

Fights and Stunts: It is always a good idea to use movement and action in sections of open air theatre.

MUSIC AND OTHER AUXILIARY ART FORMS

Of all the different branches of expression, music is to me the central and living art.

I have very rarely produced a show without live music, but music needs to be planned carefully to blend professional skills with any local participation. There is no part of a community show that forbids involvement, but be warned that badly played music will not be tolerated by any audience. The average person experiences so much music in their lives that the audience comes to expect a certain standard. Music is often the central artistic glue and like the technical side of theatre must be very well produced to provide a proper infrastructure for the community to express itself. In the plan of the show I often put a song instead of dialogue where a boring wordy lecture about some political or social point can become, in the hands of a skilled song writer, a powerful call to the heart.

It is important, too, to look into other artistic factors needed in the construction of the theatre piece. The visual images, stunts, dance, movement, masks, costumes, props and sets are just some of the components one might need. It is important to preplan every part of the entire performance in design, costing and staffing.

The Right Blueprint

When all these factors have been considered a plan is finalised and is taken back to the community for comments and reaction. At this stage it is important to get the show's blueprint 'right' as it can still be changed. From this point on it gets even more difficult to make major adjustments and any structural mistakes will cause huge problems later on.

The last aspect to work out is the budget in relation to the plans. Putting aside the subject of fund raising aside for the moment, one must draw up a budget accurately based on the updated income as it is now known. This can be difficult as one part of a theatre budget can be the income at the box office, which can be hard to assess in a given community situation.

There is the added problem with open air events that because the theatre space is being prepared from scratch, there are a lot of unknowns and these can result in budget blowouts. The budget must be updated carefully and with people with experience in such matters. Financial disaster can ruin the efforts of even the best show leaving debts and unpaid wages, harm to individuals and in some cases the potential for damaging political criticism.

If the community approves and the budget seems realistic then the show goes into production. The next step is recruitment.

RECRUITMENT AND CASTING

Barry Jones and Drunken Murderers

Recruitment is a delicate business. I have heard politicians comment that the people are apathetic and have no interest in their own future but this is simply a myth. I have found few to be apathetic when faced with the chance to express and communicate their ideas in a lively and enjoyable way. But there are various techniques in getting people involved. Find where their particular talents and interest can be used to full effect and then design around these abilities.

The place to start in most projects is the source of energy. This can lie in many places with a dynamic individual, a group of tenants, a youth club, the elderly or the community's children. But it is often the young and the elderly that have the most time and who usually want to get involved. Many projects start with a lively group of pensioners or under-twelves. Another group is often the teenagers who retain their hopes, romance and energy and can throw so much energy and enthusiasm into the making of theatre.

It is sometimes a good idea to recruit local leaders into the show at some level even if it is in a cameo role. A 'cameo' is a role in which the performer comes in for only one or two brief appearances and is sometimes just written in to give that actor a chance to do 'their thing.' Local leaders are busy and usually do not want hours out of their day spent rehearsing, but if it is quick to rehearse and does not involve lots of lines most people will participate. The fact that this person is in the show is good for the confidence of the community and it is also good that local leaders stand with the area they represent. It may be the local minister or politician or a well known celebrity that lives in the area or once did. Barry Jones, the then Australian Minister for Science, kindly agreed to be in a show we were producing in his constituency, St Albans in Melbourne. He was a child prodigy and has a phenomenal store of general knowledge. On the first night of the show the kids were firing questions at him on all sorts of subjects from Egyptian Pharaohs to Melbourne Cup winners when it was his turn to go on. I realised with horror he had not learnt his script. However, he launched into an excellent speech of his own which was just right and wowed the crowd. Politicians are never stuck for a word!

However, in another show that shall remain nameless the local mayor agreed to play a cameo roll as a murderer. He did not have much available time for rehearsals but his part was small and I was not concerned. On the night of the dress rehearsal he turned up and while I was briefing him I noticed that his eyes kept wandering. It then struck me that the man was drunk. He was weaving from side to side waving his murder weapon which happened to be a knife. 'I'll kill him, kill him,' he kept muttering. I was appalled for, if it had been anyone less than the mayor, I would have asked them to go home and recover. But here was the show's main patron stumbling about with murder in his eyes. We got through that night and before I left one of the cast said, 'If you think tonight was bad, it's the sheep sales tomorrow and then he really gets stuck in.' His wife advised a minder for the day which we organised and the night of the show he could at least stand up. So there are perils in the local leaders being cast as murderers especially if they like a drink!

There are all sorts of existing networks in a local community that can be approached and participation discussed. It is wise to discuss the show and likely participation before deciding definitely the way they can help. This allows the producer and the group to discuss its most positive contribution before decisions are made. The show must be designed around the people in a community and not the other way around.

One network can prove to be tricky in artistic terms and that is the local amateur dramatic club. They sometimes feel that, being the most experienced, they should have preference when parts are being chosen. They also sometimes bring with them bad theatrical habits which can include tantrums, emotional blackmail, backbiting and a lack of team sense. They approach the work with bad theatre techniques which can intimidate the local people. I stress that this is not always true and I have worked with excellent and courageous amateur theatre companies but community theatre is not the same as traditional amateur work and the two should not be confused.

Another tip is that people only have certain times for rehearsal and asking them to come at other times can dissipate their enthusiasm. If scenes or sections can be designed to include people who all share a certain time slot then it prevents frustration in the rehearsal period.

Casting

Casting goes hand in hand with recruitment and can be a very sensitive process. As community theatre is essentially different in process from conventional theatre the structure of auditioning people is not necessarily the best approach. The audition is helpful when a script is developed at the start of a project and there is a need to select performers to take the parts. But when the show is being designed around the people who constitute that community then the script is the end result of the process, so another approach is needed. The people are not in essence being asked to act out a part in a play but to act out a version, be it fictional, of themselves. Therefore casting is a question of looking for people who have a natural presence, a particular skill or even just the enthusiasm to take part, then putting the show together with them in mind. One point to remember is that it is not necessarily the vivacious and outgoing people that are the best performers but often the quieter ones who channel their expression through a part.

Drama workshops are excellent ways of bringing the talents to the surface and can be used as a constant reference to the community's feelings. It has often happened that after a workshop, when people see what the whole thing is about, they can direct the artists to people who can help them best and the whole network starts to work for the production.

It is startling to watch the emergence of talent. Time after time in the community one comes across people who if ever given the opportunity could make the arts their profession. They have never been trained and this can give their talent a fresh power that comes straight from their own creativity, which can be so strong in a performance. I have even in rare cases seen real genius emerge, given a chance to blossom. But there is creativity in everyone which is simply never tapped and it is always a powerful experience to watch it come out in the individual. It is not an exaggeration to say that this release of creative energy changes people's lives and gives them a new direction. The idea, (so under-developed in our society where the creed of winners and losers is so dominant), that each individual has a creative well within them that can be tapped to bring about extraordinary and positive change is clearly demonstrated in this field. It is this factor which gives so much satisfaction to the process of theatre.

There is also another group to be recruited in the community who are just as important as the actors and musicians. They are the administrative and technical helpers. In conventional theatre the space is already set up with physical resources such as offices, staging, lights, box office, sound systems and prop and costume making spaces. There is also an already existing human infrastructure of costume and prop makers, publicity people, stage managers, technical staff and administrators. They also have the advantage of a reputation with which to attract an audience.

In the community none of this is there. The whole structure has to be built from scratch each time. For this one needs help from the community on all these levels. They rarely have the expertise or experience. This brings us to the crucial point in the formation of this type of theatre and that is the choice of the professional team.

THE PROFESSIONAL ARTISTIC TEAM

To produce good community theatre one needs a very skilled group of professional workers. The professionals produce the basis of the show on which the local people will perform. They can be actors, administrators, publicity experts, musicians, visual artists, dancers, lighting and sound technicians, pyrotechnic or costume designers or a whole host of other specialists. They must be excellent at their jobs and able to understand their craft well, be able to pass on skills to inexperienced people, to work in a close knit team, deal with social involvement, work with constant consultation, to have a firm sense of social commitment and to be very creative people.

It is very hard to find these types of artists and technicians as there is little to no training being offered in this field in spite of its wide employment opportunities. The graduates of drama training establishments are ill equipped to deal with theatre making outside of a specialised environment: for example, lighting technicians might be able to move lights about brilliantly in a theatre and work a computer lighting board, but ask them to rig a lighting system from scratch in the rough conditions that sometimes are faced in community theatre and they are unable to do it.

Sometimes the teams working on shows are large, perhaps up to thirty people, and, in special cases, maybe, in excess of a hundred. This takes a good administration system and excellent communications. Usually a team meeting is needed each day to spread ideas, solve problems and share information as well as constant meetings in smaller groups. This method of meetings is excellent for problem solving as the team approach to a problem puts as many creative minds onto it as possible. But of course there has to be a balance, as there can be so many meetings as to leave no time for the project itself. The day I spent with the San Fransisco Mime Troop was spent in an all morning meeting about three lines of script. They produced only one show that year. Always have an efficient experienced chairperson who is good at keeping a meeting relevant and positive. Put a time limit on the meeting and stick to it. Conversely, we are ready to spend some time on situations which the team feel are important. This is especially true if someone has serious concerns about what is happening. The team must never get the feeling that their problems are being avoided.

The individuals in the team need to enjoy the communities in which they work. They must find the sub-culture interesting and creative or else the artistic result contains no celebration of the community. A belief by the team in the community's ability to succeed is vital, for a lack of confidence by the professional team is detected by the local people at once and leads to a poor morale. This is not always easy. It is sometimes very difficult to maintain morale when conditions are socially difficult and the people who are in the project are suffering badly from the conditions in which they live. It is at times like these that the training and professional nature of the team show through in their ability to survive the downturns as well as the successes.

THE SCRIPT

If a script is used in the theatre piece then it is essential that it is a good one. It is the foundation stone on which the rest is built but in community theatre there are many problems to be faced in the development of a well written play. In community devised work the role of the writer becomes difficult to determine and had to depart from the traditional model where a writer sits alone and builds up a script. Some professional companies employ a writer to work with the actors, research the area, speak to the local people, then go off and write a script. This can be performed by the company to local people or by a combination of professional actors and the community. Other theatre makers depend on a writer to help them build a script after the local people have evolved a scenario. It is a delicate business and many writers have difficulty in this process as they are used to creating their own work in seclusion from their subject matter. The very form of theatre is often different to conventional theatre and poses a whole new world of challenges to the creative script writer.

I often feel that the writer's involvement in community theatre becomes similar to the writer's role in cinema where the words are often adapted as the process goes along. This can be very frustrating for the person involved and needs to be explained to the artist before they start. However, I believe with training and experience we can produce good scripts which can work well as theatre pieces but also act as the channel for the community to express itself.

If there is no writer to be found with the relevant skills the way we build up scripts is in improvisation with the local people. It is in the formalisation of their spontaneous language that a script can emerge. The performers get together to work out scenes and the whole show is thoroughly workshopped. This does three things. It develops the group into a trusting, cohesive dramatic team, it teaches skills and it develops a script. It is from these workshops that the artistic ideas flow. The skill as a theatre maker is to be able to develop these ideas in the right way, to stimulate further ideas and language and the greatest possible sense of theatre; to draw out the natural performers and give a good basis for their part and to design the characters and the action to compensate for actors who, although they want to contribute, find performance difficult. An important tip in building up a show from improvisation is that the first time a scene is worked on can often produce the best work and therefore it is important to record the initial session and to use that as a base.

TECHNICAL MATTERS

The lights are planned, collected and put up, as are the sound systems. The costumes are designed, material bought, actors measured and costumes made up. Posters, handouts, adverts, press releases and all sorts of associated publicity matters are worked out and implemented. Visual images, props, special effects and space design are drawn out and built as well as music conceptualised, composed, arranged and rehearsed. All this must run to strict deadlines, tight budget control and a common artistic theme and harmony. It is in the cohesion of these multiple tasks that a good show emerges.

ASSESSMENT

Learning From the Process

As I have stated elsewhere in this book, it seems to me that a successful result must always be the aim of any piece of theatre, whatever its style and wherever it is performed. One must never use the excuse that the process was good but the show was bad, except where extenuating circumstances such as weAther have intervened. A show that does not work has Somewhere along the line it has been misjudged and the arts team must acknowledge their responsibility as artists and face up to fact that it did not work. All too often bad artistry has been covered up by examining the process rather than the product. It is vital to look at the process and the product of each show and assess what really happened. This is not to assign blame but to learn from what went wrong and to be able to improve the result next time.

Many things can go wrong in the process of a show. Faulty research can lead to bad dramatic interpretation, unskilled at workers can make a show feel unstable, the community are sometimes unable to handle their share of the responsibility; these are only some of the ways a show can go wrong and so the process of feedback has to be handled in the right way. There are two major parts to this process.

Debriefing

This is the process which allows the direct team working on the show to express their feelings about the project. It is a vital part of any production as it allows each member of the group to express what they felt went wrong and how it could have been avoided. This gives the group member a chance to express concerns and also allows detailed information which enables improved methodology.

But I would stress that this must be counterbalanced by an examination of what was successful in the project and why. The debriefing can become a very negative experience as group members can feel criticised and attacked even for work which might have been very successful. By discussing the negative points of a show a feeling of failure can emerge in the group which is completely unfounded. The process must be chaired by someone with experience of facilitating and it is usually better if that person is from outside the group. Discussion should be kept to professional aspects of the show as personal feelings completely outside the situation can sometimes emerge. But usually these sessions are very positive experiences which result in better projects.

Assessment

Funding bodies, local communities, festival committees and many other groups often want to be able to assess the theatre project after it has finished. This is not at all like the debriefing session which seeks to improve its next performance by examining what has just happened, but rather a look at the theatre show and a judging of its success from outside.

It is sometimes more difficult to assess theatre which is performed outside of a purpose built theatre because there are no constant determining factors. The theatre company may be working with a difficult community or have faced various problems which are unknown to anyone watching the show. There is also the point that the definition of what might make a good cultural product within the world of conventional theatregoing public might be radically different from what makes a good cultural product outside of that group. So in assessing any piece of theatre the following guide lines might apply.

Difficulty. The show must be assessed in terms of the conditions it worked in. Some show are much easier than others and the 'difficulty factor' might not be recognised by the audience. Like diving at the highest level it is assessed not only by its technique but by its innovativeness, courage and originality, in other words its 'difficulty factor.'

Popularity With the Participants. Was participation plentiful and enthusiastic? Was it a happy and worthwhile experience for them?

Popularity With the Audience. Did they enjoy the show? Was it well attended?

Audience Reaction. The question must be asked of the audience for whom the theatre was designed whether they felt it had made its point.

Community's Feelings. It is important to ask the original client if the project has fulfilled the aims set out in the blueprint.

Development. Has theatre been seen as a good vehicle for communication? Has it been seen as something of worth and to be further developed?

Records. One last but important point in assessment is to keep a record of the whole event, through its process and the completed show. This can be done with video, photography and\or by notes. A good recording process is an invaluable resource.

I turn to Ronald Harwood in his wonderful study of theatre, *All the World's a Stage*:

> The playgoer comes not to understand a play but to experience it. ... If we needed a test of theatre response, it would be judged not by analysis but enjoyment ... There is not one form of theatre ... If a play works, it is valid!

And Now the Show

One now has the professional team, a community commitment of people and resources, a plan for a good space, a workable budget and a scenario. Now the project can move into the last phase—production—the success of which depends very much on the quality of work that has been done up to this point. The next two chapters describe a number of productions in detail.

FIVE

■

Case Histories

Plays survive in the mystery of the imaginative world they create and its continued availability to the special community which is formed when one group of men and women ... suspend their ordinary selves to become actors, and another group finds its minds well tuned enough to become an audience. People do this for pleasure, not instruction. If a theatre does not please you ... you do not go.

RONALD HARWOOD
All the World's a Stage

Looking Below the Surface

The last chapter outlined some of the factors to be considered in setting up theatre projects in a community. I would now like to lay out a number of case studies to demonstrate examples of how these factors were resolved. The types of community in this chapter are geographical. The types in the next chapted are defined in other ways.

I have chosen four urban examples and two rural projects which give a wide range of situations and end results. I have outlined projects that were difficult and some that were easier, some that produced excellent results and some that struggled.

I am going to start with a very difficult project to demonstrate some of the problems that can emerge.

CASE 1 — ASCOT VALE, VIC.

A Difficult Situation

Ascot Vale Housing Estate in Melbourne was made up of 4000 people most of whom were non-ethnic, one parent families living in low rise flats. The local community worker, Jan Black, had formed a tenant's organisation which had raised money for a theatre project. West Theatre Company had been the resident regional company and was the obvious choice to help and at that time I was working as their artistic director.

In Ascot Vale housing estate the one parent family units at that time approached 50% of the population. The children soon grew into teenagers and hit the streets and suddenly there was a disproportionate number of young people with no facilities for dealing with their specialist needs. The other large section of the housing estate's population was the elderly. The mix was terrible, especially when there was an ethnic component of South American refugees added for good measure.

Going In

There was no community centre and no space to rehearse or perform. The 'brief' from the tenants' group was to stage a piece of theatre that would consolidate the local action group and renew confidence in the residents that they could achieve change. They also wanted to revitalise their campaign to have a centre built. There was also the fact that the production budget was low.

It was obvious that the show must be outside and even be rehearsed outside. Therefore the script would become minimal as untrained performers cannot project their voices well in that situation. The large number of young people must be catered for and this would perhaps alienate the elderly population. The teenagers were very aggressive and from the start resented our 'invasion'. On the plus side we had the full time help of an excellent community worker, Mark Grant, who had a very good relationship with the local community.

We discussed a parade format which would lead the audience around the estate and at certain points stage parts of an overall show. The audience would see a section outside the 'wash houses' where tenants clean their clothes or on top of a set of flats or in the middle of the playground. This form would provide an exciting atmosphere and be able to directly comment on people's lives in the estate.

We also decided to put up a tent to form a focus for the project and to live on the estate for the duration of the rehearsal. The form seemed exciting and gave leeway to different parts of the community to take part. But it was not to be.

We asked the local young people to help 'look after' the marquee on the project. Yes, they said, no worries. The army donated a tent and it was erected. Within an hour it had a knife rip and was covered in indelible graffiti. It was obvious that if it stayed up overnight it would be destroyed. Down it came and back we went to the drawing board.

We could not pursue the parade form as the project would be spread over the estate and security would be impossible for technical equipment. If the marquee was attacked in an hour what would happen to valuable lights and sound systems spread over the area?

We decided to form a focus and to concentrate the event in one area, but what could it be?

Circus Stunts and Gangs

The answer to one problem often comes from the solving of another. The local teenage boys were determined to sabotage the project but the younger kids from about twelve down were very enthusiastic. We started to work with them on physical skills based on circus: juggling, stilts, acrobatics etc ... Every day after school dozens would arrive and practise for hours with the dedication of trained performers. This was where the energy lay and this was where to base this particular project. We formed a circus show and rehearsed the cast in this format. We built raked (sloping) seating and formed a circus environment without a big top. This format allowed the young people to show their skills and give theatrical scope to construct scenes about the estate. It also allowed the non-theatre going audience to feel at home going to a show of this type. The form had dictated the theatrical style.

It is often vital, in situations where residents are living in bad social conditions, to demonstrate one's commitment to a project and to get a real feeling about the community one is working with. Some of the team, including myself, had made some enquiries to find some accommodation so that we could stay on the estate for the later part of the project. There was no room anywhere and the idea of caravans was mentioned. We followed up the idea and parked two caravans on a spare bit of ground outside the tenant group's flat. But although this brought us closer to the residents we also became targets for the local gang.

The community had often been promised help, but it had rarely materialised. We wanted to signal to the local people our involvement by staying there while we worked and, in doing so, gain their help and trust. But the local 'boys' perhaps felt we were invading their turf and went to town to try to break us. They would arrive at night and sit in our caravans and we would feel that we were getting somewhere. Then when they left they would throw stones or rock the van with us inside or bash it with sticks. It was very difficult. They would be positive one moment and negative the next. I found it very mystifying, for however tough the young people had been in similar areas they had always come through. But not these kids. We did not somehow fundamentally understand their needs and responded in the wrong way.

On to the Show

The next stage was to develop content for the show. In this case it was very difficult. We had an exciting form but its ability to be more than just a circus seemed to be limited. As far as the younger kids were concerned the circus was enough but we now had adults involved and they wanted to perform something with more meaning.

But the techniques to perform outside, where actors use large gesture and good voice projection, were beyond the present skills of the local people. We built up scenes with strong visual appeal such as a scene with the local tenants being treated like circus animals forced to jump through hoops, in other words building up the circus as a metaphor for the people's experiences.

It was near Christmas and the local people wanted a Carols by Candlelight event. I was sceptical about the idea but we organised a Salvation Army band and made dozens of beautiful lanterns.

The fact that we were working outside with no security made it all the more difficult and the constant trouble with the young boys was wearing us down. It seemed that to get any show on at all would be a victory. To attract the local people to the show and fill the five hundred seats, we organised an afternoon fair. The concept of theatre is foreign to most people living in these conditions and the piece of theatre must often be disguised in a form more readily accessible to the general public. In this particular case the local people would relate to a festival and then their interest would be aroused to come and see the theatre. But this meant we were having to organise a festival as well as the project. However, there was a lot of enthusiasm for the festival and it came together easily with schools and other local organisations putting together different events.

We put up the frame work for the circus type seating a couple of days earlier and just seeing the thing coming together was a great lift for the local people. But we were still under siege in terms of theft and vandalism from the gang.

I remember the night before the show sitting in the caravan and feeling like early settlers in America in their wagon train surrounded by Apaches. I felt that perhaps the whole program had not been worth it and went over in my mind the series of decisions that had put me in a caravan in the middle of the Ascot Vale housing scheme. I questioned whether this was theatre in the real sense of the word and whether we had changed into social workers.

The next day we started at dawn to rig the show, as none of the equipment could be left overnight. It was a lovely hot day. The fair went well and every one of the six hundred seats was filled with people who had turned up to the area's first ever celebration. At half past seven the show began.

The space looked lovely and gave a good setting to the performance. However, the show was a technical nightmare. Each time we put down props they would be stolen or smashed by the young boys and the cast simply sat with their family in the audience. The order of the show was totally upset by the fact that no one could see the point of rushing about with split second timing. I was distressed.

Half way through the show one of the team, John Bolton, with whom I had worked for many years, said to me how well it was going. I was amazed that he could say that. But I saw his point. Every seat was filled and the audience was obviously enjoying it tremendously. The local people had no preconceptions about the way a show should be performed and were not judging it on the same criteria that I used as my guide line. This was their show and it was working on their terms. There was a communication of emotion and understanding. I consciously relaxed and began to enjoy it too.

At the end of the show a twelve foot high puppet, internally lit with candles, moved across the stage and was seen as the rekindling of the Ascot Vale spirit and their determination to organise their way out of the social difficulties that plagued them. It was a beautiful moment and a powerful one because, although the situation was so desperate, the people still held out hope. I announced the Carols by Candlelight and expected most of the people to leave. Not so.

Most of the audience brought out their candles and lit them and the lanterns were lit and held over the band. For the next forty five minutes the people sang those ancient songs about the birth of Jesus. It was beautiful and as someone told me afterwards the first time that the community had sung together.

What Else Could We Do, Be Nice?

It had been hard work and I felt that it had not been what outsiders would call theatre at all.Yet it had been as successful, theatrically speaking, for them as any bit of theatre in the conventional world could have been in more normal conditions.

Conventional theatre has evolved a gauge for quality and a way in which it judges theatrical product. This is, of course, only relevant when the criteria are the same. If the cultural base is changed the criteria for judgement must change also.

We packed up the show and counted our material losses with everyone helping. We finished about one o'clock in the morning and one of the boys, who belonged to the local gang, came up to me and put his arm around my shoulder and said, 'I thought what youse lot did was okay.' 'Why', I asked, 'did you try to destroy it all the time?' 'What else could we do, be nice?', he replied.

The next day Mark Grant and I had seen that the rubbish was put away and piled up a mountain of garbage to be collected by the council. As we sat in the office looking out of the window the young gang swept out from behind a building and kicked the pile all over the oval. Mark and I looked at each other in desperation. They had the last word. We went out and slowly piled up the garbage knowing that while we were leaving the estate those kids were not and that was their comment on that fact.

So what had the theatre project achieved?

It had not managed to connect with the young teenage boys but had involved the children and some of the adults in the show. It had not achieved a high standard of theatre in the ordinary sense of the word but it had produced and event which contained true community expression. We had been struggling with the making of a good space but had we really made the correct decisions as regards the mounting of a production?

Three things occur to me in retrospect.

The first was the very fact that something was achieved by the people to express their community. I believe that theatre had galvanised this feeling in a way that nothing else could.

Secondly it had brought out hidden problems and now the community could at least face them rather than allow them to remain under the surface.

The third was the effect it had on certain individuals in the area and the way in which theatre can build personal confidence which was later to lead to the emergence of local leaders at a later time.

A Good Event—But Is It Art?

A question remains though: in this context, what makes good theatre? The process, however beneficial, can never be the only part of community theatre. It must also produce a good result. The theatre worker must make a good piece of dramatic art that works in the context. I felt we had failed in this case to achieve the movement from an event to theatre. Yet in the light of later developments I was to see the local people take on theatre again and this time they took it another step forward.

The story of Ascot Vale was not by any means finished. Our company kept up communication through the coming months and this, of course, is the advantage of a theatre company geographically situated in the area in which it works. Two years later the local people raised funds to produce another show and invited us to organise it.

But now many changes had taken place in the area. What a difference!

The community centre was now built and the tenants' group was working on all sorts of levels and bringing about a large number of improvements. The young people we had worked with in the last project had grown up into teenagers and the group we had had difficulty with was not around anymore. The situation was a delight to work in.

People were very enthusiastic and constructed the story with the theatre team. It was based on a theme of people leaving home, experiencing new situations and discovering new feelings about their community. The local adults build a spaceship to escape the problems of everyday life and leave the young people in charge of the housing estate. Two stories ran parallel with the characters finding themselves on strange planets that resemble the different strata of our own society and the kids having to face the responsibility of organising the local area themselves. The two groups learn much through their experiences and when the parents return the community is united again but is now much stronger.

We built the same sort of raked seats and performed with them in the new community centre. We had good audiences but because it was inside there was not the same visual impact of the first year. To balance this we organised an open air dance after the show to which everyone in the community was invited. Again the work of community theatre often goes beyond the strict barriers of just organising theatre. The project had gone well and had laid the foundation for the future.

CASE 2 — KENSINGTON, VIC

An Urban Problem

This was a project that was funded from a number of
different sources to bring the aged and the young
people together in a fragmented community. The event
was to be held in Kensington in Melbourne which is a
mixture of conventional housing and Ministry of
Housing estates. The worst aspect to this area is that it
is on the main truck route through Melbourne which
pollutes the atmosphere and physically divides the
community in two. The route goes through the main
shopping centre and this dislocates the main meeting
place in the community. It is also split socially by
different social groups and ethnic divisions.

The idea of bringing together the old and the young
came about because the local community school was
doing a social survey about the elderly in their area and
found out that the contact between the young and the
elderly was non-existent. One of the teachers was also a
City of Melbourne councillor and felt that a theatre
project might bring them together.

The Old and the Young

We received funding for the project from Melbourne's
Youth Festival (The Next Wave) a philanthropic trust
(The Myer Trust) and Arts Access who are a Melbourne
based arts agency who deal with the disadvantaged. We
began to look for a space and, as it was winter, the
space had to be inside. We examined a good many
which included the local town hall, schools and various
other possibilities and made up a list.

We also started our research and found the main focus of the aged to be in a club at one end of the area. A focus for youth was the Kensington Community School which was the school that had done the original research at the other. It was clear within the first day that although the project had been funded with the best intentions the actual community had not been involved. The elderly said that the young people were to blame for much of what was going wrong with the area and the young people said that the elderly were 'boring'. It seemed impossible to bring them together. If we chose a space where the young people lived then the elderly would find it difficult and if we chose a space where the aged gathered then it would be equally disastrous. The whole project seemed inoperable but we felt there must be a way.

One factor helped swing the balance. It was that the two groups *did* want to perform although not with each other. This at least allowed us access to energy and permission to start on the project. Now the question was how we could design a project that would bring them together at least physically if not dramatically. We thought that if the groups could see each other's work then bridges might be built towards a better understanding.

We felt that if we could design the space to allow for maximum informal contact and yet could facilitate the needs of both groups to perform in a formal fashion then the project had a chance. The only space big enough for the numbers of performers and audience involved and also available for the time required, was the local community centre which was adjacent to the Ministry of Housing flats. It was not ideal as it was not central to the area and very much tied in with the flats. However, we had no choice but to adapt this utilitarian hall which was more suited to sports than theatre.

We started to ask the groups what they would like to take on in their performance. The young people wanted to put on two short plays. The older group wanted to perform a play about pollution in the environment. (In this area there was, and still is, a high pollution figure and there are constant chemical fires and explosions.) They wrote a play about a chemical fire disaster and how it affected the area. The younger group wanted to do a show about their day dreams and what would happen if they came true. The elderly, on the other hand, felt they wanted to do a series of sketches about love and emotion. Now we had the makings of a project.

The Vital Moment

We had therefore three short plays and the moment of decision had now arrived. In each project there comes what I would call a 'vital moment.' It is the moment when a decision is made or thought is expressed that a whole project will hinge on. In Ascot Vale it had been the caravans and in this case it was the designing of the 'right' space and support system to make it work. The hall had a stage, but that formal presentation would not have worked well. One logical answer was to create a warm, exciting cabaret space with the audience sitting at tables, the band on the stage and the acts on a small projected dance floor. Now we needed to develop a theme.

The Dream Cafe

It was the younger group that sparked off an idea. It was the notion that dreams could manifest themselves in reality. The space could be a place that manufactured people's fantasies and so the Dream Cafe came into being. The theatre company's actors then became the staff of the Cafe and could, in character, support and link the community's plays. Cabaret had become the theatrical form. A plot was worked out to tie the whole thing together and a script written by a professional writer.

It was a simple plot about the owner of the Cafe inheriting money, leaving it to the staff who are all desperate for cash for one reason or another. They then spend the evening trying to kill him. In between the murder attempts the community puts on the shows. The space worked on three levels.

Firstly it transformed the community centre into a luxurious night spot and took the audience into a new experience which was removed from their normal lives. Secondly, it gave an excellent platform to bring people together both in the cast and in the audience as the performers sat at various tables in the space and mixed freely. Thirdly, it allowed the professional team a good form to be able to support the inexperienced community actors if they needed help. Therefore, if an old person needed physical support on to the stage the 'staff' helped them or if the young group needed props the help was built into the theatrical structure.

To build up a cabaret atmosphere we rigged black velvet curtains around the entire hall, put in rostra for some of the audience tables and chairs, rigged a sophisticated lighting system which operated between lengths of white parachute material, decorated the whole space with images and organised dozens of pots of greenery to give atmosphere. In contrast to the space, the theatre shows themselves had few props and no sets and were performed in the dance area in the middle of the audience. The space was creating the right atmosphere and so the theatre could remain simple. The tables were covered with fine linens, vases of flowers, a carafe of free wine, highly polished glasses and bottles with lit candles in them.

The show was packed every night and the space worked very well. In contrast to the project in Ascot Vale, the setting up had been trouble free and the young people very enthusiastic. The young people's shows went well as did the elderly sections and the two groups watched each others' work and, I believe, got a better understanding of each other. They mixed freely in the informal atmosphere and built up relationships. A bridge had certainly been built in the community and both groups had expressed their concerns and their dreams.

This show turned out to be a celebration of the people in the community and the warmth and co-operation that had been achieved in the project had been very satisfying. I had no doubt about the theatrical value of the piece as the form had created the means of expressing emotional beauty. One scene in particular comes to mind.

The aged had, as I have said, took love as their theme. To express their feelings about it they had written various scenes from the great lovers of history, Anthony and Cleopatra, Adam and Eve and others. Jan (Meme) MacDonald, who was directing the elderly cast members had cast a newly married couple as Romeo and Juliet. They had been married for only one year but the man was aged eight-five and the woman eighty-two. They were wonderfully gentle people and went through a ten minute version of the famous play with the help of the 'staff' of the cafe. The beauty of these two people, who were reaching the end of their lives and who obviously loved each other, playing the death scene was one of the most moving pieces of theatre I have ever seen.

There was a theatrical spin off in another direction which no one foresaw at the time. The centre itself had been very influenced by the event both in its form and its emotional impact in the community. Under the guidance of an energetic community centre leader, Paris Aristotle, the centre has continued to produce community theatre to great effect.

CASE 3 — ST. ALBANS, VIC

Designing Theatre to Meet Local Needs

The project came about in Melbourne in the suburb of St. Albans which has one of the highest migrant populations in Australia. In 1982 we had done a project about the migrants in a circus tent with a large cast. The local people then held a winter festival and asked West Theatre to stage an event. The budget was low and another large scale production was not possible. There was no suitable inside area to work in. Again, it was a question of how to design theatre to meet local needs.

One of the local residents mentioned bonfires which had been part of his old country's traditions and this gave us an idea to stage theatre around a creative set that would then burn as a bonfire. The example had been set by Welfare State International in England who staged large scale bonfire theatre by building a scaled down version of the British Houses of Parliament and burning them on Guy Fawkes Day.

Burning Your Boats

An idea was born of building a large scale old fashioned sailing boat to represent the migrants crossing the oceans to Australia in search of a new life. I had discovered in my previous research that most of the original migrants in the area had been refugees from the Second World War or the consequences of it. The Maltese had their islands destroyed in the war and in the economic depression that followed many had been forced to search for a new future. The Italians likewise came from the south of Italy whose economy had been wrecked by the fierce fighting in the invasion by the Allies. The Greeks had come over after the civil war in their country in 1948 and the Yugoslavs when the communists took over. Another interesting group was the D.Ps or Displaced Persons who fled from the Russians westward over the borders. These refugees arrived in western Europe in their hundreds of thousands and some had made their way to Australia.

The area has people from almost every country in the world, as new emergencies in other lands brought new refugees to Australia. The world's miseries might well be measured by the country of origin of the immigrant who arrives in St.Albans.

The local councils were very helpful. They collected the waste wood from the area and instead of putting it on the dump they left it for us in a large piece of waste ground in a factory area. Slowly a large boat was built, and it measured sixty metres long and was made of two hundred and fifty tons of wood.

We built up a story which took the form of a myth of two characters who leave war torn Europe in the boat and experience all the perils of the sea to arrive at their new country. But as part of their agreement to come here they must promise to burn the boat upon arrival.

The figures had to be seen from sixty metres and therefore had to be large scale, so two fourteen foot puppets were built and worked by six people. The sailing boat was decorated by local schools who made beautiful sails and other images about the sea. Visual artists constructed the props needed for the story. A sound system was rigged near the audience and lights were put up for the show. A script was written and the music planned. The whole piece was then rigged with fireworks, smokes and pyrotechnic effects to bring the show to life.

The night of the show various ethnic groups made food and organised dancing before the show and the audience of over a thousand gathered for the performance. Amid fire and smoke the story unfolded to music and the voice of the story teller. The great puppets emerged from the smoke and explosions of war torn Europe and climbed onto the boat.

The ship was led in its journey through plague, famine and pirates by a mythical whale who was eventually destroyed by torpedoes from a nuclear submarine. The migrants arrived and celebrated with a rocket show, but then had to fulfil their bargain by burning their boat. They had to relinquish the past to embrace the future.

The bonfire was duly lit by local M.P. Barry Jones and the whole ship burned, which took many hours. It was a spectacular and moving sight and we hoped the audience remembered their own struggle to get to a new country and the loss of the old which the burning represented. But I am sure for the younger people in the audience it meant something very different and perhaps gave them an opportunity to experience a new way of celebrating from old cultural roots.

CASE 4 — WILLIAMSTOWN, VIC

Scapegoats

The last of the urban examples is a show of a different kind where a community wanted to put on a show for the general public.

The community was Williamstown which is a quiet, village like area in Melbourne. It is where the old port used to be situated in the nineteenth century and still retains an atmosphere of old world charm. In the middle of this area of relative economic wealth there are Department of Housing flats which live on a kind of social island. The estate was being attacked by some local councillors who claimed that their area should not have public housing. They felt that they should not have to bear the responsibility of housing anyone and the area should be for private housing only. It was the attitude of saying yes, we recognise that there are problems in the world but we will exclude them from our area.

These councillors complained that 'the flats', as they are called locally, had piles of rubbish lying about. The facts of the matter were that the area where the flats were built was a common short cut for everyone in the area and the rubbish that you would find on any footpath was not cleaned up by the council because it was claimed that it was housing land. All the residents' rubbish had to be put in large skips outside the flats which in the summer were a constant source of flies and smell. Another complaint by these worthy burghers was the noise late at night under the flats. The noise did exist because the roadway through the flats was at the back of many of the pubs and it was the emptying of these pubs of people from all over the area that caused the trouble rather than it being the residents' fault. In fact the flat dwellers were the main victims of all this trouble. In other words they were being made scapegoats.

The flats were adjacent to a park which was the site of an excellent local festival which is attended by people from far beyond the area. The residents wanted to stage a piece of theatre that would balance these attacks being made upon them and reverse the image of the flats as being a bad place.

A Theatre to Communicate Beyond the Community

The major skill in all theatre, which is repeated so often in this book, is to bring the right show to the right audience at the right time. In this case the community wanted to present a product to a general public audience. They would be under severe pressure to come up with a product that, in artistic and in political terms, would be accepted. Again, the form was a key factor. It had to be outside, and it was important to get it right.

On an open air stage with microphones the cast would be at their weakest because that form restricts action and calls for precise techniques that even professional theatre performers can find difficult. It ended up in the circle format which needs careful staging because the audience are not just in front of the actor but all around. But a circus project the previous year had taught the young people at least the basics of this sort of performance. So the form in this case was fairly straight forward.

It was the story that had to be just right. It was delicate, for too much criticism of the council would lead to a more negative situation and yet the residents wanted to make strong comments. We turned, as so many have in the past, to metaphor.

Rats, Weasels and Birds

The eventual story which was worked out by theatre workers and local residents was a sort of Animal Farm, concerning a weasel and a rat who live in a lovely spot and believe they have a right to all of it. A flock of birds arrive and ask the animals for a part of the land. The rodents refuse to let the birds settle. The birds protest and claim that the weasel and rat do not own the land and therefore they have the right to live there too. The weasel and the rat try to get rid of the birds by various means. They try to make their life intolerable by constantly wetting their living quarters, send in thugs to frighten the new tenants, send in drunks to give them a bad reputation. But their efforts are to no avail and the birds overcome their problems and banish the rodents for their greed.

Another important point was that the quality of performance must meet the expectations of the general public. The commitment of the tenants was wonderful and they worked very hard to achieve the highest level of performance possible. The young people especially were producing excellent performances and executing feats of skill.

The show ran each day of the three day festival and was performed for large audiences. The show contained circus, puppets, song, music, comedy, acrobatics and very little dialogue and on one level it was good entertainment for the festival, but of course, on another, it was saying a great deal about the situation.

But it was also saying a good deal by the very fact that the show was happening and being performed well by the residents. It was clearly demonstrating to the town in general that the residents of the flats had the concern and the talent to show their worth in public and to stand up and be counted. It was very important that we, as a theatre group, did not let them down in such a public arena because if the show had failed it would have further reinforced many of the townspeople's views towards the flats. This is a clear case where the theatre workers must be totally responsible for the work that they do, as failure can be damaging.

Urban communities can be very diverse even within the city of which they are a part. However rural communities, from which these next examples are taken, have a very different feeling about them. They are generally more closely knit, and people tend to know one another well. Once the community have backed the theatre project they can achieve a great deal as resources are local and everyone knows where to get them. Spaces too are much easier to find and many rural areas have good spots nearby.

CASE 5 — KATHERINE, NT

Sometimes theatre, however well planned, comes short of one's expectations. At other times for no reason that one can discern it turns out superbly well. Theatre has its own internal force.

Katherine is a small town of four thousand people lying about three hundred kilometres south of Darwin in the Northern Territory. It is surrounded by harsh, dry bushland and the climate is inhospitably hot and dusty for much of the year. The town is to some extent a focal point for social problems among both Aboriginals and white people. In addition, the Australian Air Force has built a large base ten miles from the town where over two thousand personnel live. In other words there are many potential sources of social friction.

The Northern Territory Arts Council funded a theatre team to organise a show in the town with the aim of bringing these differing parts of the community together in an event.

The first task was to find a space which would be suitable for a show but would also give us an atmosphere of conciliation. The local Arts Council representative, Wendy Fahey, and I visited various sites but it was the river that was most interesting. The Katherine River is a wonderful place with deep, clear green water flowing through a landscape of tropical trees and flowers. The river is life to everything in the area and symbolises beauty and strength to the population whatever the colour of skin or political belief. The show had to be held at the river.

Knotts Crossing was the original crossing place for the Aboriginal peoples and the early white explorers. A small dam formed a deep green pool on one side and the dam itself formed a natural stage for theatre. The river crossed the dam in a small waterfall and made its way in a gentle stream across the crossing area. On one side was a beach of white sand and on the other a shore of small pebbles. The site contained several smaller settings each of which had its own atmosphere. Its isolated situation made power a problem, but who better to solve that than the Air Force who are well used to working in the bush. We visited the air base and borrowed enough generators to give us the power we needed.

Now we had to design a show that would bring people together in a place that, although beautiful, had no real focus for performance. One form which suggested itself was a festival of theatre with a large number of small events spread through the space. The audience would move at random throughout the area to watch whatever took their fancy. This would give us the advantage of using the area's natural strength, also allowing us to work with conflicting community groups in isolation from each other while still bringing them together for a celebration on the night.

This form was a good one, but a central theme was needed. We had a meeting of all the adults that were interested in the show and one suggested the idea of a perfect society. The show was called Utopia after Sir Thomas Moore's book. Each group was asked to use this idea as the theme to their theatre piece.

All sorts of groups rehearsed their small performances and it was especially interesting to work with the school children and with their view of the perfect world. The classes had many Aboriginal children in them but they were very reticent and withdrawn and were really not part of what we were doing. However, we decided that we would go across the river to the local settlement and work with the children there. The local community leader was very helpful and we planned a series of workshops. When the young people were out of the school and in their own environment they changed radically from quietly subdued children to laughing bundles of energy. We worked with this group every day and formed some real friendships.

About one hundred people rehearsed their performances and into these formal shows we put various other theatrical parts. We planned a large scale finale where the local people of our 'Utopia' would appease the crocodile spirit with fish so that the community might be free from attack the following year. We also formed a choir, set up a piano on the dam, built hundreds of lanterns, formed a little bower where a Wise Woman could tell fortunes, planned lantern lit canoe rides and organised various musicians to play impromptu. The night arrived and we lit several hundred candles at the top of the road for the audience.

It was a little way out of the town and we had no real idea if the local community would come, but within quarter of an hour we had about eight hundred people gathered. The cast were carrying fire torches and lanterns and at the right time we marched down the road toward the crossing. We had all come up in day light and now the whole area was laid out in the darkness.

Hundreds of candles, fairy lights and lanterns reflected in the river and transformed the area into another world. The atmosphere was magical and it was not hard to imagine that for this one night we were truly going to 'Utopia'. The space was working for us in a very strong way and this helped the theatre product.

The Aboriginal young people performed magnificently in front of a white audience some of whom might normally have little truck with the black population, the local policeman played a nasty civil servant trying to stop the event, the local lawyer walked on stilts, a choir sang anthems of peace and a hundred other small events made up the evening. Hot foods and cold drinks were served to audience and actors alike as people took breaks between different events. The Wise Woman had a queue all night of people who entered a little enclosure lit by candles and whispered their secrets and asked for advice.

A pianist played Chopin on a piano covered with candles as people sailed across the water in lantern lit canoes. A bush band kept the audience lively and dancing as the evening drew to a close.

But, however beautiful the evening had been there had not been an event which had produced an image of real theatrical power. This was to be the climax of the evening. A sixty foot image of a crocodile carried by nine people emerged from darkness escorted by flaming torches, drums and whirling smoke. It threatened the community but was appeased by two young girls who feed it magical fish to return to the river. This ceremony might seem fanciful in the safe confines of Melbourne or Sydney, but in the Northern Territory where people are killed and maimed by the crocodile it takes on a new meaning. Of course people living in 1988 in Katherine do not take this ceremony at its face value. But the experience does create within the audience a renewing of the relationship between ourselves and natural danger.

The people of Katherine had created a vision of a perfect world, a vision of what they wanted from their society. It had provided a window through which they could share a common aspiration and during the evening the community had proved that with a common will and creative thought they could tackle the problems that faced them in their day to day lives and celebrate the strengths already existing within their town.

CASE 6 — IONA, SCOTLAND

The Holy Isle

The last example of rural theatre turned out to be only a week in the preparation but the results were very special indeed. This was on the island of Iona in Scotland and the performance became a celebration of the human spirit.

In the life of a theatre director one hopes that most shows turn out to be good, workable productions that fulfil the brief given and are popular with the audience. Now and again there are disasters, not often one hopes, but they happen. But every now and again there comes a show which is filled with magic; a certain combination of events which produce, as if by accident, an extraordinary experience that makes up for the others.

The island of Iona is on the extreme edge of the West Scottish islands that pepper the Atlantic. It was where St. Columba landed in 563 AD to bring Christianity to the Scots from Ireland. He built a rude shelter and started his ministry which was to eventuate in the conversion of Scotland. His house is now a mound of earth and front of it there has always been a church of some sort. It was, and still is, a place of great significance to the Scots and for hundreds of years their kings and queens were buried there. At the end of the last century the abbey was all but a wreck, but slowly through the first half of the twentieth century interest grew to restore the building.

A non-denominational religious community was formed by the Rev. George MacLeod in 1938 and people of all descriptions, including artists and craftspeople, came from all over Europe to work on it. Strange pieces of good fortune accompanied the work such as the freak wreck of a timber boat during the war which gave the Abbey its roof. Another strange occurrence was the arrival of a group of white doves, from no one knows where, which now nest in the building. It is a place where these sorts of things happen. The Iona Community is now a loose knit group of people from all over the world who subscribe to certain values and beliefs which I would describe as a broad caring attitude based in Christianity.

The area that I was working in at that time was Easterhouse which is a very large and poor housing commission in Glasgow. The local arts organisers, Grace and Keiran Grant, were asked to run a training week in the Arts for sixty people from all over Europe.

Many ideas were put forward to give the visitors a good experience. It was decided that one of the best forms of training was to all work towards a show and in doing so everyone could learn new skills. However, there was no chance to set up the project beforehand as no one knew the composition of the group.

We set off on a Saturday morning with two days to spend before everyone arrived. To get to Iona one takes a ferry from the west coast of Scotland. The boat lands on another island, Mull, a bus crosses the island and then at last another ferry brings one to Iona itself. The moment I landed on the island I had felt the strong and powerful atmosphere in the place. It is filled with a strange energy. It reminded me of the physical power of Uluru (Ayer's Rock) which far outweighs its size or shape.

Walkway of the Dead

We had one day to construct the project. I was taken along the Walkway of the Dead which goes from the Abbey to the graveyard and learnt that this was the route the funeral processions took when they carried Scottish royalty to their resting place. The grave yard itself is small and the markers of the ancients' long since gone. My guide explained that the bodies of dozens of kings and queens were now inextricably mixed up in the graveyard. He started to tell me some names and suddenly one jumped out from the others. Macbeth. 'Macbeth!', I said, 'surely not *the* Macbeth!' My guide said, as he pointed to the green Celtic cross that stands proudly before the Abbey, 'Macbeth saw that when he visited the island in around 1046.' Well, I said to myself, there can be little doubt as to the theme of this project.

To rehearse Shakespeare's play in a week was, of course, impossible but the themes of the play were wonderful to use as a structure. But with so little time, the utilisation of sixty people's enthusiastic energy was no mean feat. To complicate matters the local island population, whose daily lives are linked to that of the Abbey, had heard about the show and wanted to become involved. Upwards of a hundred adults and children were all rearing to go to stage this 'simple' production. We quickly made out a 'skills and interests' chart which asked people what they could offer and what they would like to learn. The composite list was staggering. Here was a group from many different backgrounds and cultures who had gathered because they were interested in the arts and their context in society. By the very nature of the group this produced the collective power to achieve a great deal. The 'simple' production had within the first few hours become a project capable of great sophistication. As in other community shows, the 'person hours' that can be spent, even in the span of a few days, can be huge.

In this case there was an arts team of eight, a training group of sixty, six in the staff of the Abbey, all willing to give at a conservative estimate ten hours a day for six days. This totals 4,440 hours of creative work and this does not include the energies of the local people.

With this sort of enthusiastic energy combining together it was a matter of focus. This meant forming different groups to work on 'their' piece of the show and to work hard on making sure that these parts made a harmonious whole. An orchestra was formed and a choir who were given various tasks that included set pieces linking music and choral effects. The group of costume makers tackled the tast of clothing a hundred people for the show and making all the various flags, banners and decorations. Rehearsals were started and the different scenes built up, scripted and learnt. There were publicists making posters, teams on props, large scale image makers, stunt fighters, pyrotechnicians, administrators, acrobats, writers and composers, all working in their own fields to create a whole. The feeling of mutual work and direction was infectious and liberating. Rousseau said that there is no communication as pure as the silence shared by common work. As each day went past the excitement and enthusiasm grew and the island's special atmosphere fuelled the energy level.

Burning Missiles on St. Columba's Mount

The six days went by in a blur of action and activity and yet there was a feeling that time had slowed up and one had been there for months. Rather than sum up the process I would like to record the event. A resume of Shakespeare's version of Macbeth might be useful. He starts the play as a young baron who has just repulsed the Vikings from the Scottish shore. He meets three witches who tell him that he will become the king of Scotland. When he arrives home he learns that the Scottish king, Duncan, is coming to visit. He and his wife plot and kill the king and inherit the Scottish throne. Lady Macbeth, filled with guilt, kills herself and the tyrant king Macbeth is deposed and killed by MacDuff who has led an army against him.

On the Saturday night at dusk, which in the northern regions of Scotland can take some time, the audience and cast, which numbered about four hundred, gathered at the jetty which faced the Island of Mull across the water. As they looked over the sea a boat set off from the opposite shore. At first it was indistinct but soon the crowd could see that in the bow stood a Scots figure holding a flaming torch. Behind, a bagpiper played the traditional melody of the crossing to Iona.

The king of Scotland, Duncan, sat midships surrounded by flags and banners. The scene could not have been far from the sight that greeted the eyes of the islanders so long ago when the monarch visited the holy isle. A choir greeted him when he landed and when he was welcomed the whole parade set off for the Abbey. The procession went up the hill from the villages and, as it passed through the ruins of the old nunnery, in flashes of smoke the three witches appeared to confront Macbeth. While the audience heard their dire predictions the king did not and when the witches vanished the crowds started to warn the king of danger. The show had become a living experience.

The parade arrived at the Celtic cross outside the abbey and suddenly the Vikings streamed over the hill in an attack. Macbeth beats them off and Duncan, unknowingly, fulfilled the witches' prediction by promoting Macbeth. It was now getting dark as the audience and the cast moved into the cloistered area of the abbey to watch in the light of hurricane lamps the murder of the king by Macbeth and his wife. The choir and the actors combined to form an atmosphere of evil and malice as the drama unfolded. Macbeth was proclaimed king.

Suddenly the main doors of the Abbey were thrown open and the crowd entered the mainly part of the beautiful church which was lit mainly by dozens of candles. There they witnessed the coronation of the new king and watched as his tyranny pulled the country to bits. He summoned the witches to bring his power and was taken by them to hell. The emergence of the devil in the church and Macbeth's total spiritual disintegration was incredible. Macbeth was given a Nuclear Missile, (these were being built in Scotland by America at the time,) and now was in ultimate control. But, his corruption complete, he was disposed by MacDuff and equilibrium restored. The missile was picked up the cast and processed down the aisle of the church to the orchestra playing Brahms Requiem. The spectre of nuclear war and the threat it possesses electrified the church. The theatre had now become a force of its own and I am sure that anyone in the abbey that night will never forget it. The missile was placed on St. Columba's mound and a child put her hand inside and released white doves and the bomb was burnt. As we all stood there watching the symbolic end of nuclear weapons we were filled with a hope for the future.

The theatrical experience had galvanised the night and I am positive that each person felt that the power of human co-operative action can halt the world's destruction.

SIX

■

Specialised Communities

While you sleeping
you dream something.
Trees and grass same thing.
They grow with your body,
with your feeling ...

Those trees ...
they grow and grow.
Every night they grow.
That grass ...
no matter it burn.
When it drink
it grow again.
When you cut a tree,
it pump life away,
all the same as blood in my arm.

BILL NEIDJIE

ETHNIC THEATRE

The first of these specialist groups is the ethnic community which is defined by the country and culture of origin rather than a geographic location, even if its members live in the same area. In Australia there are ethnic communities from every country in the world. I may say that ethnic identification is a very delicate business. One might think that the Italian community share a common culture yet Italy has only been fully united since 1879 and each region or even village feels a separate identity.

Another dynamic is that the older generation who were born in the original country hold mayonto their culture yet the children who have been brought up in Australia have now taken on a different set of values. This causes friction in the home and an inner conflict within the young people about their cultural heritage.

I was asked by FILEF, an Italian community aid group, to do a show. FILEF was being funded by the government which at that time was controlled by the Labor party. The local branch wanted to do a show based on the Eureka Stockade which they saw as the birth place of a multi ethnic Australia. They believed that the gold rush had brought people here from all over the world and this had brought about the beginnings of the ethnic mix we find today. It so happened that Raphael Carboni, an Italian, had written the only comprehensive eyewitness account. There did seem to be links and in fact the young people who wanted to be involved were from a multiplicity of backgrounds and cultures. But the theme was lost on most of the people in the cast as their real link with Eureka was in fact nonexistent. In retrospect the show would have been better to have been about Italian culture in Australia, based on personal experiences.

(Another show was done by FILEF in Sydney, directed by Robin Lawrie, which did this very thing with excellent results and an account of it is in 'Community Theatre in Australia' published by Methuen.)

Theatre workers need to find a cultural guide and that person can act as a bridge between the ethnic culture and the artists involved. I have heard the criticism that theatre teams should not work with a culture that is not their own, and one can appreciate that point of view, but I believe it is essential for the development of a rich culture for ethnic groups to work and cross fertilise with Australian artists regardless of ethnicity. The projects need not be seen as cultural theft but the use of one culture to enrich the other.

Celebration of Welcome

The potential of cross cultural work was made apparent to me when I went to the Vietnamese 'Tet' Festival in Footscray in Melbourne. There were thousands of Vietnamese there and I realised that most of the Vietnamese population in the city was present. However, I was one of about a dozen westerners who had discovered the festival by accident. All the publicity was in Vietnamese and there was no information about it in English. When I asked an organiser about this he said that it would be a waste of time as Australians would not be interested in the festival. Yet here was a festival which was incredible in its richness and diversity. The food, the dancing, the theatre, the singing and the music were wonderful and compared with the average local suburban festival it was a feast of culture.

I was working in the area with West Theatre and we decided to approach the Vietnamese community and ask them if they would like to work with us on a project. The Australian historian Geoffrey Blainey had at that time been alerting the country to his fears about Asians in Australia. The Vietnamese we were working with believed he had focused a great deal of negative attention on Asians and it was in this atmosphere that we started our project.

The Vietnamese are not immigrants in the usual sense but are mostly refugees. They fled their country after the communist victory and waited in refugee camps hoping for resettlement.

The actual approach was very difficult because of the suspicion that had been built up in the Vietnamese community. Some were very helpful but others did not feel enthusiastic.

We were helped by poets, actors, musicians and singers who would be considered to be highly competent in their own country and yet worked on taxis or in restaurants here. We also worked with young people who had just arrived in Australia and were living in a hostel and were glad of the opportunity to join in an activity in their new country. We also approached local schools in the area and asked for help. One young man, An, turned up one day saying that his school had told him about us. We asked him what he would like to do and he proceeded to astound us with a blur of circus skills including juggling and acrobatics. He told us he came from a family of circus performers who had survived in the refugee camps by entertaining the people and now lived in Australia. Eventually the whole family became involved and were the greatest of help.

Another group that wanted to help were the students of the local college who were very keen to show their culture to the general public and gave us a lot of advice and support. It was through the students that another group became involved, a team of youngsters that practise a form of Vietnamese martial art.

We now had over forty people who were willing to join with us and we were lent a local theatre in which to perform. However, planning the content of the show was very difficult. The story material was plentiful and everyone that took part had stories to tell of their hardships and struggles, but the language was a real problem with only four people speaking English and none of us talking Vietnamese. There remained a difference in culture which separates the West from the East and this was always with us. It is difficult to explain but the emotional heart of the people's experiences was only revealed occasionally. The show had to be designed to be understood by both Vietnamese and Australian audiences and this limited the ability of the actors to convey emotion. There was lots of skill and spectacle but the heart of the project had not been reached. It was asking a great deal and the mere fact that we all worked together was a great step forward. There was however one outstanding breakthrough. On the night of the dress rehearsal there was a scene where a mother must say goodbye to her family as there is not enough money for her to leave on the boat with them. In other rehearsals she had waved and gone through the motions but on this particular night she suddenly started to dance to the music which was a traditional song of parting. The dance was very simple but expressed all the pain and suffering that so many people had gone through.

We used an interesting technique to bridge the language barrier. The Vietnamese actor who played moon godess, talked in Vietnamese and repeated the words spoken in Australian by the Australian actor and vice versa. Therefore the script was being said in both languages. The Australian knows nothing of Vietnam. The Moon princess told the story of a family from Vietnam who escaped as boat people and eventually

Aboriginal elders begin the Arafura Games with a traditional firelighting ceremony, Darwin, 1991. *(Photo: N.T News)*

Children carry candlelit cockatoos in the 'Night of a Thousand Lanterns', Arafura Games, Darwin, 1991. *(Photo: Jude Swift)*

Monkey, symbol of Brunei, Arafura Games, Darwin, 1991.
(Maker: Techie Masero. Photo: N.T News)

The Elephant, symbol of wisdom for the people of Thailand, Arafura Sports Festival
Opening Ceremony, Darwin, 1991. *(Image: Neil Cameron. Photo: N.T News)*

Fish swimming, Pacific School Games, Darwin, 1992. *(Photo: N.T News)*

The sun, Pacific School Games, Darwin, 1992. *(Photo: Jude Swift. Image: Faridah Whyte, Paul Lawler)*

ABOVE: Maleny Folk Festival
Fire Event – 'the Tower of
Babel', 1992.

RIGHT: The Sun, Pacific School
Games Opening Ceremony,
Darwin, 1992. *(Image: Faridah
Whyte, Paul Lawler.
Photo: N.T News)*

The Gates of Renewal, Maleny Folk Festival, 1993. *(Photo: Jeff Dawson, Complis)*

The Wicker Man, Knox Festival, Melbourne, 1988. *(Photo: Neil Cameron)*

The Coming of the Sun, 'Seeds of Fire', Alice Springs, 1993. *(Image: Neil Cameron. Photo: Centralian Advocate)*

'Seeds of Fire', Alice Springs, 1993. *(Photo: Centralian Advocate)*

The rainbow, 'Seeds of Fire' Alice Springs, 1993. *(Photo: Centralian Advocate)*

Neil Cameron. *(Photo: Centralian Advocate)*

arrived in Australia via the refugee camps. The story went on with some of the experiences that the refugees faced in Australia. Some were serious but some were very funny. For example one of the Vietnamese actors told us that when he had arrived in Melbourne he had seen 'no standing' signs and thought this was a very repressive government that did not allow its citizens to stand on the pavements.

The shows were well attended and it was good to see the Vietnamese and the Australian audiences sitting side by side enjoying this joint project. Parts of the show were made into a television documentary about the story of Vietnamese refugees.

The research and the involvement of the Vietnamese was the longest we ever had to do and still we had only scratched the surface. It is the same in the research of all cultures foreign to oneself but if the show reflects the shared experience and opens our eyes to the thoughts, histories, images and art of other cultures, then it must surely be worth it.

THEATRE IN THE INSTITUTION

People in an institutional setting can include the intellectually and physically handicapped, the blind and deaf, the mentally ill, inmates of prisons and young offenders units and patients in hospitals. Each one of these communities has its own specialist needs and the teams that produce theatre with them need to be well resourced and experienced. Yet the theatre can be not only of great benefit to the groups by giving them a chance to communicate and express their experiences but also produce theatre of great power and emotion. One need look no further than the excellent theatre of the deaf produced in many countries or Aldo Genaro's work with the mentally and physically handicapped in

Australia or Dorothy Heathcote's work with young
offenders in England.

The reasons for these successes are simply the needs of
all people for an avenue of expression. But what makes
people in institutions different is that the system that
they live in often produces a situation where usual
forms of expression and communication are denied
them and this leads to a serious situation of deprivation.
The best example I can give is an experience that I had
in a hospital for the deaf.

Ten years ago, while I was living in Scotland, there
was a deaf school which denied the children the use of
sign language because they felt that it inhibited the
development of speech. Our theatre team went into the
school to teach drama and to help the children express
themselves through movement and mime. I have rarely
seen such a burst of emotion in any group as in these
students. The students had been denied the means for
physical expression for so long that the classes were an
explosion of emotion and this sometimes expressed itself
in anger. The head teacher told us that we could not
control the class and we were upsetting the children. I
remember on our last day one ten year old kid
pounding the desk with his fists in total frustration
when told we were finishing. It was a terrible
experience to see the human mind trapped by its own
body. There is a happy end to this particular story as
the school was taken to the European Court and the
authorities forced to implement a more sympathetic
system.

Working with the Mentally Ill

EXAMPLE NO 1. To cover the work done by different
artists in institutions would take a book in itself and
there are various works available. But I would like to

describe two projects which give some idea of the problems and the rewards. These were at Larundel Psychiatric Hospital and the St Vincent Boys' Home.

Larundel

Arts Access, a Melbourne based arts agency who have done a great deal of work in this field, asked West Theatre Company to organise a project at Larundel Psychiatric Hospital in Melbourne. We planned a project around the long term patients who were there from several months to many years. We made it clear we were a theatre company and definitely not therapists. We did not want to enter the hospital with the attitude that we could help cure anyone. If our project had beneficial effects that was good, but our major responsibility was to develop pieces of theatre. We wanted to explore theatre and its limits and had confidence in the situation but we felt that the project must be built on a strong foundation. We could not just arrive and expect the staff and patients to understand what we were doing. John Bolton and Linda Waters, who were part of our team, worked for one day per week over ten weeks doing drama with the group and when it was felt that there was a solid group we then brought the whole theatre company there for a concentrated week.

In keeping with our policy of trying to live within the community, the company moved into the hospital for the week and stayed in some empty space in the nurses' hostel. This proved to be a key decision as we had a chance to experience first hand the feeling of an institution and this proved to be essential in understanding the feelings of the patients and staff.

The head of the hospital, Dr Barlow, was very supportive and helpful and allowed the group full freedom. Most of the staff were eager to help and the ones that disapproved of the project kept well clear.

I was personally very nervous about working with the mentally ill as I did not know what to expect. After I had the chance to settle in and meet the patients, I realised that they were as nervous as we were and I began to feel a bit more comfortable. The mentally ill are not as I imagined them to be, which was some vision of white gowned people running wild in cage-like wards. My view of madness was based on a stereotype and in the coming days I was to radically change my perspective. I believe that our reluctance to work with people who are different and are institutionalised is often based on our own fears rather than the realities of the situation.

The group, I am sure, realised our nervousness and gave us a warm welcome and made a real effort to make us feel at home. There were about nine patients in our temporary theatre company and eight theatre workers and we all sat down to discuss the week. After a talk we discovered that the patients throughout the hospital have no entertainment in any form and so a plan was worked out to take small theatre pieces to every ward in the hospital. We split into two groups with patients and actors in each and spent the first two days rehearsing the short shows which would tour every ward in the hospital. We would also work on an evening's entertainment on the last night where all the resident patients could come along and enjoy a social evening and theatre presentation.

Jumping Mouse

The team I was with produced a twenty minute story based on an old American Indian myth called Jumping Mouse which is about a young mouse that hears a roaring noise in his ears. His family and friends call him mad. He leaves home to discover the source of the sound and, in a long journey, discovers wisdom. The story was very popular and the audiences loved the relationship between madness and discovery. As the days progressed many of the patients told me of their 'madness' and in many cases they had seen visions that, in other ages at other times, would have been considered profound. I am sure that William Blake if he lived in Melbourne in 1987 would have been in a metal institution.

We ran improvisation classes each day and they were fascinating. Some of the patients had trouble with their inner dialogue and their imagination. There had been a breakdown and it brought them to the institution and yet it was through their mind that they must find a way back into society. It was felt that the process of learning to trust their imagination again is critical in the process of getting well.

The improvisations were great for freeing the imagination and having fun with ideas although the reaction was often unexpected. One of the most remarkable things was that the patients played out scenes of their lives and these were incredible to watch. What was curious was that everytime they played mad people they shouted gibberish and waved their arms about. This was in marked contrast to their usual behaviour which was quiet and restrained. One of the patients explained that was how people saw madness and so that was how they acted it out.

We ran physical warm up classes each day and on the first day started with only a handful of people. Within a few days the numbers had increased to fifty. It was really popular but quite unlike our usual warm ups. The patients could not in some cases even lift their arms above their heads and found even the simplest stretch difficult. No one was forced to go beyond their capacity and each day saw an improvement. It was as if their bodies had been locked their body in a frozen attitude of tension and the warm up was freeing the muscles. It was certainly doing good and the patients kept coming. I felt that these classes could go a long way to bringing back a feeling of well-being.

We took shows to every ward every day and to get to them we paraded with the actors and the patients. The bringing of life to the wards and the energy of performance cut through the deadly routines and predictability of life in an institution. The community is a mix of staff and patients and the experience of life outside seems far away. The patients have little with which to compare their behaviour and it is difficult to recover in an atmosphere where the only companions are other mental patients. Their use of outsiders to bring about change and stimulate the environment seemed vital.

The Black Diamond Cafe

We converted one of the large rooms into a good space using the model of a country bush dance and called it the Black Diamond Cafe. Everyone in the hospital was invited to watch, dance to the music, perform and present theatre in an atmosphere of friendship and support. One hundred and fifty people came and we had great support from the staff, some of whom were good performers in their own right. The drama group put on the work it had been performing and the products were full of humour and a great deal of sanity. At the end of the evening the whole audience and cast, patients and staff, danced and sang in an atmosphere of fun and were bonded together in a mutual feeling of celebration.

The patients had been very interesting to work with. They had been unfettered by the usual and normal ways of approaching theatre. They had no expectations and therefore the theatre that was produced was wonderfully original and interesting. I learnt a great deal about how we fall into the well worn ruts of conservative presentation.

Arts Access has run other successful projects in the hospital since then.

Theatre With Emotionally Disturbed Boys

EXAMPLE NO 2. The second case history is again in Melbourne at the St Vincent Boys' Home. This is an institution run by a religious brotherhood. The staff is in the ratio of one teacher to three boys. This may seem high but the young people are very difficult to handle and emotionally disturbed. What this means in practical terms is that some are violent to each other and the staff, few will respond positively to any given situation, they do not necessarily respond to their teachers and they are prone to very anti-social behaviour. They are also very vulnerable to their peer group and many spend time in a great deal of misery. Our team decided to become resident for a week and work towards a show although in this case it was not appropriate for us to stay on overnight.

Elephant Men

The youngsters suggested many ideas for a performance but one suggestion jumped out from the others, the idea of 'Elephant Man.' Here was a perfect story to dramatise with the boys, as the elephant man's rejection by society was not unlike their own. It also had a positive ending where John Merrick, in the film *The Elephant Man*, became accepted by society.

The whole school suspended curriculum work and the staff, our team and the boys worked full time on the show for a week. It was terrific to have the support of the staff led by Brother Elmer who, with infinite patience and understanding, led the situation to a good conclusion. The first day was good. Five hours with the boys was wearing in the extreme and I think that in spite of a one to one situation the team finished the day exhausted. Every step forward was countered by two back but we had achieved some progress. The next day went very badly.

The students reacted very violently and it seemed impossible to achieve anything. If a boy did something positive the others would try to disrupt it. They were constantly fighting and breaking the equipment and running wild throughout the rehearsal.

The third morning was very bad and a dramatic production seemed far off. In the afternoon we had our first dramatic run-through of a scene and quite suddenly the students watched each other's work with quiet attention. I decided to keep the show going and with everyone watching went through the first half with the cast improvising. I think that by running through the show the boys had begun to see what might be possible. The students were also learning circus, music and visual arts and in these sessions we got to know the boys as friends. The boys were fearless at physical work and seemed to have no fear of hurting themselves. With this attitude they quickly mastered acrobatics and put on a real turn of skill. As individuals they were very affectionate and demanded a great deal of touching and hugging and once the trust was built up, they showed a great deal of humour.

After five working days the show was as together as possible under the circumstances. The show was organised for 7.30 in the evening and friends and families were invited. All through the day the youngsters were getting more and more nervous and I began to realise that they had a great deal to lose emotionally by performing in front of their families from whom they were desperately seeking approval. The crowd gathered and the space filled to capacity of about seventy. One of the students who was a great little actor, waited by the door for his mother for an hour before the show. He told me it was very important to him that she saw it. At the last minute I said to him that we were going to start and he reluctantly came in and his mother never arrived.

Before the show the theatre team agreed not to place pressure on the situation with our expectations but no matter what happened to give support and show that we were enjoying it. This was vital. The whole show developed a style of its own and was wonderful. The team gave away the set criteria for slick theatre and embraced the real theatre that was being presented. The students were very good and the audience love it. The whole show took on a power because everyone understood the courage that the students were displaying by telling their own story and, as so often happens in community theatre, the reality of the actors situation becomes the emotional power of the piece. The youngsters were stunned after the show as people congratulated them and we all felt that they had taken a step forward together and proved something to their parents and friends.

We packed up and said our goodbyes. As I was leaving I remarked to one of the staff that it was a pity that the mother of the boy had not turned up. The social worker told me that she had died three months ago and the boy could not accept her death. When love is denied, the world becomes a very desolate place.

PROJECTS IN THE WORKPLACE

The next community to be examined is the community of the workplace. We have performed in factories, mess halls, offices and staff rooms. The most memorable setting was a slaughterhouse where a hundred employees watched the show dripping in blood!

This type of theatre is very specialised. The shows must be relevant and designed to fit into all sorts of spaces. The length of the show is critical as workers have only a set time to watch. The Melbourne Workers' Theatre is a professional company set up to take on all sorts of issues which concern the worker and bring these issues to the surface with music and humour. But there are other ways to get involved in the workplace. Theatre projects can be based in the workplace and integrated into events in the factory.

A sugar factory in Melbourne held a festival for the workers each year where the factory was closed down for a half day. We were asked to become resident for a week and work towards a performance at the festival. This was more difficult than it sounds as the workers were tired and did not feel like adding to their work load by rehearsing theatre. There was also the problem that the management did not want criticism from the workers and this produced a form of censorship.

We made some progress but the result was not very satisfactory and, whereas it did liven up the workers festival, it did not give the people who worked in the factory much sense of meaning.

One of the most spectacular examples. I have seen was a project produced by Jan (Meme) MacDonald when she was working for West Theatre Company in Melbourne. The show was called 'Vital Signs' and it was produced by SIGNAL, a branch of the Nurses' Union.

Signals

The nurses' union at the time was fighting a running battle for all sorts of improvements in their working conditions. An arm of the union, SIGNAL, was interested in constructing a play based on the issues and hoped that it would inform and educate the general public.

Jan felt that it should be performed at the very heart of the workplace, in the hospitals themselves. She got permission to put on the show in two of the major hospitals in town. The tension between the nurses and the medical system was very high and the whole issue was taking on national importance. Performing the show in the hospitals would bring the whole issue into the limelight and it was hoped would make the show very accessible to the nurses and build a feeling of confidence and energy in their strength.

The decision to perform in two hospitals meant that a theatre space must be built from scratch in two places rather than one. This meant an awe inspiring amount of work for the production team who then had to rig front of house, lights, raked seating for five hundred, sound systems and a whole host of other things all within the week of production. Yet it was necessary to do this if the show was to reach the right audience.

There is a real pleasure when one is working with a community that is keen to communicate its ideas. Forty nurses were involved directly in the performance and many others assisted in the production. For them to then get involved in long hours of rehearsal after a day's work takes real commitment and this was not lacking in this group. In spite of late shifts, family and other commitments they turned up and gave their energies to the full.

The nurses all worked on different shifts and it was very difficult to get them all together for rehearsal so the show was split into three separate parts to accommodate the different work times.

The Three Parts of 'Vital Signs'

The first part was about witches and their relationship with the nursing profession. The play put forward the idea that women who lived in the dark ages and explored healing were often persecuted because the church thought it was interfering with the will of God. The emergence of the medical profession excluded these women healers.

The second story brought to life the world of the nineteenth century nurses who were nothing less than slaves and in spite of their experience were treated as totally medically ignorant.

The third story brought the audience to the modern day where those nineteenth century ideas were still being exercised. We see a world where the nurse's day to day care brings them into intimate contact with the patients. We also see another world where administrators and doctors make some devastating decisions about the patients when they have had little to no contact with them. A lovely song which finishes the show is quoted here in part.

Nursing has been my beloved,
I'd die for it, I demand it,
I've searched for it out of little grey days,

But it's the nights, It's the days,
When a doctor says your slip is showing,
As Mrs Smith is dying and your back is splitting in
    two,
I've been an honoured custodian,
Of your last precious secrets,
I've uttered so softly 'fore death steals you away
But it's the days, It's the nights,
When someone wants to hold you truly,
You hide your tears you cannot say,
That he'll never be home again.

I say that I'll hold your hand,
Like when you were so small,
I'll be your mother, your lover,
I'll be the last face you will see.

                                    Song by Robert Eastcote

It was a fine piece of theatre packed with nurses each night although I think few doctors or administrators attended. It had managed to be good dramatically, involve the community and get over the point about the nurses' situation.

THEATRE IN SCHOOLS

Reaching the Student

The school can become a powerhouse of cultural development and learning for the whole community if there is enough vision.

At present theatre in schools takes four main forms: drama classes that in some schools are often seen as mere frills; school plays that are performed to students and parents, usually using known scripts; professional and semi-professional companies who tour both primary and secondary schools with all sorts of entertainment which is sometimes based on an educational theme and sometimes not; and the theatre artist-in-residence in the school environment and the production of work that can result. It is this last form that will be discussed because the other forms are well documented in other publications.

There is an increasing trend in certain educational systems to open the school to its local community and to bring in skilled people who are not trained teachers. For example, bringing in a writer to talk to an English class about the skills and techniques of writing can be a wonderful educational tool.

In theatre the possibilities are endless. Artists can run workshops on a whole range of skills which might include circus, mime, lights, make up, stunts, voice work, improvisation, writing, music, song, prop making, costume work, sets and acting. But the question that is often asked is: what have these pursuits to do with finding a job and adjusting to the world?

I believe they have everything to do with finding a job. They develop self-discipline and co-operation, expand the creative capacity and build a feeling of self-confidence. They are life skills that we all need to be able to pursue our chosen direction. They teach emotional growth which is so often lacking in a purely academic curriculum. They are also fun, which is often the best base from which to learn anything. But theatre in schools can go a great deal further than workshops.

Women for Peace

This project in Footscray Girls Secondary School in Melbourne was instigated by the arts teacher. The head teacher too wanted to see innovative projects happen in the school environment. The curriculum of the whole of Year 8 was suspended for a week and we were invited into the school to run a project.

Year 8 numbered about one hundred and forty students and we had a team of seven. We started the week by putting on a show in the school yard to stimulate interest and to introduce ourselves in a dramatic form. We then gave the students a choice of seven options, each to be led by one of our team. They included music, drama, photography, circus and dance.

We asked that the teachers be involved as well so that we did not just become substitute teachers while the real ones took the week off. This worked with some who felt the project worthwhile but others felt uncomfortable because of the relaxing of the usual routine and discipline. In every institution one can get ready help from enthusiastic staff but conversely there is also often some of this resistance by others.

Young people one might meet in a social situation suddenly change when they walk through a school gate. They relate to adults in a totally different way. They relate to adults as Sir or Miss and see us very much as teachers who are responsible for their behaviour. In a project this must be broken down and the young people must be responsible for themselves and their work. This way of working is frowned on by some teachers, however it was not our job to educate but to produce theatre and our approach must be different. This is a central problem for all outsiders working in schools. For example, when the young people would express themselves in a certain way the teacher would say 'No, that's not the way' or 'That's not right,' where we were there to allow the students to express their feelings not to judge whether they were doing it correctly or not. It is well to discuss these types of problems prior to the project starting and make sure the objectives and the decision making structure are well organised and agreed upon by all parties.

It was the International Year of Peace and we decided to make that a theme across the board and at the end of the week we would present our work to the whole school. The school was in the multi-ethnic area of Footscray and the group I worked with had twenty students who spoke sixteen languages between them. They decided to do an immigrants' version of Romeo and Juliet. It concerned two neighbours of different ethnic extraction who were always fighting. The children fall in love and the families are brought together by the tragedy that follows. It was about peace and love and how they can overcome hate and the students believed that their parents must do that to live in Australia.

The students interpreted the feelings of peace in exciting new ways and it was very interesting how each group expressed a great idea of optimism about the state of the world. I am sure that the students had a very creative week and that educationally it was valuable.

THEATRE WITH THE AGED

Respect Age

Another group worth mentioning is the aged. It is always a pleasure to work with the energy of the aged. Of course, the people in this group were born before television and have a lively tradition of entertaining themselves. They also have a resource which is invaluable to younger generations and that is experience. They have lived through our own history and link us with patterns and thoughts of the past. We are quick to consign the over sixty fives to stereotypes. But not all theatre being done with the aged has to rely on the past. They also have a great deal to say about the present.

I was invited to see a pensioners' theatre company in San Francisco called the 'Tale Spinners'. I was told that they rarely performed to general audiences and preferred to reach their own age group. I was prepared for a gentle, sentimental journey into the past with songs from a bygone era but that is not what I found.

I sat down in the front row of the audience of elderly people and the show began. The cast of about twelve actors came on, formed a row and lifted their fists in a sign of revolution. The elderly in the audience all cheered and clapped. The show was stunning. It exposed the way in which society treated the aged and demonstrated what could be done about it. If society was going to treat them this way then the only people that could change it were themselves, by standing up for their rights. The director told me afterwards that the group had felt that their theatre should not look back, but forward. They wanted to express their feelings and bring about a change of attitude in themselves and their audiences.

The Tombolas are an aged theatre group based in Carringbush Library in Melbourne who are well worth contacting for further information.

WOMEN'S THEATRE

No Myth

Jan (Meme) MacDonald, who was the director of WEST Theatre Company, produced a show called, 'No Myth' about which she said this:

A phone call came in to WEST. Someone had seen *Vital Signs*. Could we do a similar production with the survivors of domestic violence from surrounding Women's Refuges? And could only women work on the production? And could we do it soon?

This phone call was the beginning of a project which challenged all those working on it way beyond the boundaries of theatre and into the darkest nooks and crannies of personal identity and behaviour.

A great debate began amongst the members of the company. There was immediate enthusiasm for working on a production with such an important and challenging theme. But women only? We were and always had been a mixed gender company. Or had we? Thinking back, WEST was named by the group of eight women who first staged a production called *Roma* in 1977. WEST actually stood for Women Essendon and Suburbs Theatre.

Precedents can satisfy the intellect but don't budge the emotions. The debate continued. The men in the company didn't want to be treated as 'the enemy' for the sake of their sex. Were women the only victims? What about the injustices on both sides of the fence? Why not construct a working situation the overcomes rather than reinforces the negative relationship of the sexes?

The emotions ran strongly around these critical philosophical challenges to what is a heartfelt need of many women to have space to be together, to be separate and to feel safe.

Cautiously at first, the women from the Refuges agreed to a basis of working whereby all the discussions and script development sessions for the production were held with women only and when it came to the physical skills development sessions two of the men from WEST assisted with their skills helping to train the all women cast in sessions that were optional.

In the context of all the discussion of ideas and theories it was breathtaking to watch women whose confidence had been stripped away, literally beaten down, struggle to meet the demands of performance. The physical challenges of walking on stilts, tumbling, standing on shoulders, forming pyramids, firek-eating, mask making, rigging lights and so on were the manifestations of a much deeper challenge. Trust. Trust that a hand offered in support can really be relied on. That the body can be a source of freedom and joy, leaping, rolling, tumbling, standing strong. That other bodies can be trusted to take the weight. Trust that others will be careful and together a pyramid of strength can literally and metaphorically be built.

The physical skills development was balanced with sharing of personal experience and the gathering of a collective sense of what story needed to be told in performance. Many women's experiences were still raw and painful. Seeking answers to why the violence continues between men and women led back into the past. Way back and then finally settled with the Greek myth of Demeter and Persephone.

This ancient myth provided a mask through which emotions could be safely played. It could also be cast aside and contemporary parallels substituted in critical moments of action. Like all good myths we could find ourselves within it and add colour and flavour at will with the freedom of distance. Above all it was theatrical and provided a solid spring board for our often shakey confidence and new physical skills. We could show off and have fun, laugh as well as tell of the torment.

No Myth was a beginning with all the strengths and weaknesses of first steps taken in any new direction. Its greatet achievement was that it lit a spark setting alight the enthusiasm and sense of worth of an enormous range of women. The performance went on to a second season in the 350 seat Universal Theatre where the eight performances were booked out.

This spark kept spreading for years. Women from the group who had never performed in their lives before formed street theatre groups, wrote and performed in experimental plays and eventually estalished the outstanding Women's Circus inspired and directed by Donna Jackson. As one of the Women's Refuge workers in *No Myth*, Donna was the driving force initiating the project and assisting me with direction.

Rather than provide answers, *No Myth* opened up a process of recovery—certainly for individuals but equally importantly for the broader community it touched. The courage of the women involved opened the way for turning the intolerable despair and injustice of domestic violence into inspiration for the theatre and hope for life.

WORKING WITH ABORIGINAL PEOPLE

River of Dreams

I have lived in the Northern Territory for the past four years and have had a chance to do projects with Aboriginal people mainly from Central Australia. It has been a fascinating experience in which I have learnt how little I know about this ancient people. It is a subtle and spiritual culture. I would like to describe one of the

projects which was organised by the Northern Territory
Arts Council in Alice Springs. The Todd River is a dry
river bed which runs through Alice Springs and only
flows intermittently. But when it does flow, it floods
and a huge amount of water cascades through the town
with little warning, sometimes drowning people, usually
Aboriginals who camp in the river. The Northern
Territory Government planned to build a dam upriver
to stop this flow through but many people, including
the Aboriginals, were against it. Environmentalists
believed that the impact on the flora and fauna of the
river bed had not been considered properly and the
Aboriginal people objected because the proposed dam
was to be built on sacred ground.

Clive Scollay who has lived in Alice for many years
and speaks the local Aboriginal language believed that a
show about the river would at least bring the debate
into focus. It was not to be a 'protest' but a show which
focussed on the river itself and people's feelings about
it.

The environment groups and various individuals and
schools wanted to take part, as did Aboriginal people,
but we had to find the right site. We wanted to perform
the show in the river bed which is powerfully beautiful
and Clive took me to meet various elders who directed
us to the right person, the Aboriginal owner of the spot
we wanted to use. His name was Thomas Stevens. He
and other custodians met us on site and told us about
the spot we were about to use. The spot was free of any
major dreamlines which are believed to be paths made
by Aboriginal spirits in ancient times and was, in fact, a
dreaming area of the small water frog.

As we walked along the river bed Thomas named each
spot and told us the special name of each tree. For me it
was a beautiful area but for Thomas it was a place full
of meaning where the world could be understood and it

was in his care. To see this land through his eyes as a precious inheritance to be cared for really brought home to me the anger that Aboriginal people felt about the dam. On the site, some builders had driven a four wheel drive onto the river bed and taken away some sand. This had killed one of the mighty red gums which stand majestically along the river. These specialist trees take many decades to mature and Thomas saw its death as senseless waste.

The story we constructed was about a destructive force that comes up the river and carelessly destroys the environment. The spirit of the river rises up to oppose it. It was vital that at all times we respected the Aboriginal culture and although the story was 'our' story we asked Thomas and others to inspect our work and look at the words we were going to say in the narration which he was going to help us with. For example, we planned to construct a sixteen foot puppet which was the female spirit force of the river, which we envisaged as female. Thomas said this was okay but the colour of the puppet had to be white and there had to be a male as well as all things are made up from both energies.

At each stage it was all checked out and eventually the show was ready. About eighty Aboriginal and white people came together to act, sing and dance in a story which we all understood however separate our specific cultures.

To discover the Aboriginal culture which stretches back for 35,000 years is a vital part of living in this country. It is a culture which would take a lifetime to explore and even then one would only have started. Until we begin to understand the dreaming it is going to be impossible to ever feel at home in this land. Part of community theatre is to awaken that dreaming and to let it enter the psyche of modern Australia.

PART THREE

■

Celebratory
Theatre

■

SEVEN

Festivals, Parades and Rituals

We are seeking a culture which may well be less materially based but where more people will actively participate and gain power to celebrate moments that are wonderful and significant in their lives, be this building their own house, naming their children, burying their dead, announcing partnerships, marking anniversaries, creating new sacred spaces and producing whatever drama, stories, songs, rituals, ceremonies, pageants and jokes that are relevant to new values and new iconography.

JOHN FOX
Paper for the English National Arts and Media Strategy
August 1991

Celebration and Culture

In Western society, live interaction with the arts has been diminished in the mainstream of people's lives.

The old festivals of life and worship of the powers of creation are now thoughtless consumer events and the use of theatre to express the important events of people's lives is greatly eroded. We are living in an ever increasing mono culture which slowly swamps our relationship with our own feelings and community. The 'culture' that we do get is a parade of non-participatory experiences usually based on other cultures far removed from ourselves but omnipresent through the domination of television and films.

The act of celebration is seen by most in the late twentieth century as a frivolous pastime, and for many, the search for meaning in existence is confusing and pointless. Yet I believe that the need for celebration is of the utmost importance to us all. The ability to enjoy on the deepest level the joys and sadness of our lives, our sense of being alive and the joy of existence with the help of others in our community, is fundamental to a society's health. And yet, how difficult Western culture finds it to truly celebrate. Peter Brook said that 'we do not know how to celebrate because we do not know what to celebrate.'

Let us look at an ancient celebration and how it has evolved into a festival of today.

Pre-Christian Scotland celebrated the harvest and the end of the growing period with a festival of thanks which was to appease the gods and bring their good favour for the next year. It also fell in with the coming of winter and was held at the end of our modern October.

It was celebrated with a large open air ritual which involved building a huge human figure out of wicker, as big as a modern electricity pylon. Inside this huge effigy were put all sorts of offerings. The whole thing was then set on fire and offered to the gods. It was the natural end of one cycle and beginning of another and so became the Scottish New Year: a moment marked, a time to reflect the past and look forward to hopes in the future, to recognise one's relationship with the soil and one's beliefs and contemplate one's mortality. It was called Sambain and served another function, a communication with the mystery of death.

Throughout festivals in human history into the present day for example in South America, there are events designed to confront the concept of death. The Scots believed the dead would return from the underworld on this special day in autumn and try to find lodgings in a human house, preferably the house in which they had lived, and in so doing would not have to return to the world of the dead. To gain access the ghosts had to get over the doorstep. The householder must stop them coming in by giving them gifts to go away.

The date became formalised as October 31. When Christian beliefs supplanted the older ones, they did what they had done to so many of the important dates in the 'heathen' calendar—they superimposed their own festival on top. The concept of a Hell full of demons became linked to the older idea of the underworld, and gradually the festival took on the characteristics of what we know as Halloween. 'Hallow' means saint and 'een' means evening and so it was the night of the Saints. It is followed by All Saints Day on November 1, where the dead could become reconciled with God. Both days are related to beliefs about the afterlife, intercession, redemption and new beginnings.

The ancient rituals of appeasing the dead at Halloween are carried on by the children who go from door to door dressed as ghosts getting gifts so that they do not come in. The practice was taken to America where it transformed into 'trick or treat.'

Just as the ancient festivals were taken over by Christianity, today commercial industrial interests have supplanted those Christian festivals. The new belief system of materialism is now in ascendancy and the meaning of the old celebrations is eroded. The Spring Hare is a good example. The mystical symbol, the hare, found in cultures throughout northern Europe, represented hope for good harvests and healthy children as Spring growth returned after the Winter. Amid dancing and celebration, eggs, which were a symbol of fertility, were rolled down a hill with a huge fire wheel. The magical hare has became the fat pink cartoon Easter Bunny which organises the gorging of commercially produced chocolate eggs. The serious act of understanding the importance of Spring for ourselves and our children is now a commercial vehicle. Worse still, the hare that represented a mystery of life has been replaced by an image of cheap sentimentality which further obscures our children's perception of the natural world and our dependence on it. Christmas and Easter, the major landmarks in our annual calendar which have symbolised birth, death and resurrection, are being separated from their spiritual base.

This is a dangerous direction as it is clear that the suppression of a people's celebrations and culture leads to the disintegration of their society and that they then become susceptible to exploitation and cultural imperialism. To deny a people their power to sing, dance, express, create, articulate, communicate, paint, write or perform is to kill their development.

My own country, Scotland, has suffered from the effects of 'cultural genocide' which has resulted in the dislocation of the Scots as a people. In 1746 the English armies fought the Scots at the battle of Culloden. The English won the battle and then systematically set about destroying the Scots' Highland culture. Their music and songs were banned. The wearing of the tartan and the use of their official language, Gaelic, was forbidden. The

unique clan system that had sustained their way of life
and their relationship to the environment in which they
lived was broken. Some were even sold to the American
plantations as slaves.

The clan system of the Highland Scots worked on the
basis of a traditional area being controlled by an
extended family. The farming of the land had been
based on the croft system where, in some cases, each a
farmer would have a piece of land that gave them the
greatest possible variety of land conditions. For example
the strip might lie from the top of a hill where the sheep
could feed down through some woodland which would
provide wood and then flatten out to an area adapted
for crops, ending on a beach where seaweed could be
eaten, driftwood used and access given to the sea for
fishing. The English troops moved in long lines through
the valleys and 'cleared' the people out. A monoculture
of sheep was then substituted to provide wool for the
big cities and the land given to large scale land owners.
The people left to find new lives throughout the world
but they had become dislocated. The culture had been
severely damaged and even today that moment still
lives in the Scottish psyche.

The parallel with Aboriginal people in Australia is
striking. The Aboriginal culture was totally integrated
with the environment in which it lived for thirty
thousand years but was suddenly dislocated when
whites arrived. The British system was imposed with no
regard to local conditions and the result was the
disintegration of the Aboriginal way of life. The
relationship with the land was destroyed and with it the
Aboriginal's central reason for living.

I believe that Aboriginal people find it difficult to
relate to a culture which they see as harmful to the land
and our attempts to integrate their culture with ours
have often been disastrous because many of the

underlying principles in our culture are in opposition to theirs. This results in a people whose culture has been severely damaged and who are ideologically, spiritually and emotionally unable to do things our way. They are in a terrible limbo which produces a disintegration of their community and personal dislocation.

But the white culture in Australia also suffers dislocation and a feeling of displacement in an environment which is not suitable for their imported way of life. The British culture had little idea of how to develop a society into this new land. It ignored the fact that the climate, the flora and fauna and the land itself were different from their homeland and invested in the European culture from whence it had come.

We have ended up with a culture that mixes European and American values and aspirations. It feels uneasy. We struggle for a new culture that makes sense to us, one that includes both the reality of the land and the people we find around us. A type of theatre has emerged in recent years which maybe called celebratory theatre is the exploration of a new, more relevant culture based on the needs and visions of the community in which we live.

FESTIVALS

Festivals are those vital events that mark our lives and celebrate our relationship to our community and belief system: the marking of special times of the year, the festivals of spiritual contemplation, celebrations of life's vitality and also the private rituals surrounding birth, marriage and death. Celebratory theatre can regenerate these events in a local cultural setting or on a large national scale and give them a new importance and significance.

Neitzsche had this to say about festivals. 'Dionysic stirrings arise through the influence of those narcotic potions of which all primitive races speak in their hymns, or through the powerful approach of Spring which penetrates with joy the whole frame of nature. So stirred, the individual forgets himself. For a brief moment we become our real selves, the primal being, and we experience its insatiable hunger for existence. Now we see the struggle, the pain, the destruction of appearances, as necessary, because of the extravagant fecundity of the world's will.'

There are many festivals in Australia which are succeeding in incorporating artists into a communal festival situation. One of the most outstanding is the Maleny Folk Festival, just north of Brisbane, which has reinterpreted the meaning of folk music to produce a New Year's Festival of world music of the highest standards. The director Bill Hauritz and his team have created a truly Australian celebration which taps real feelings of renewal as the old year finishes and the new year starts.

But many festivals we experience in modern society have lost their inner meaning. We still
want to hold them, we still have a need for them, but as traditions erode or have simply never existed, we find it difficult to find a new direction. So often the same things are repeated year after year until they become stale and tired and a sense of real joy is often generated artificially by drink.

Ironically, many festivals now focus on the arts; where once artists played a critical role in constructing a festival around a community's shared reality, now a festival must be artificially constructed to give the arts a sense of purpose.

How can theatre, in our modern festivals, show the way back towards real celebration?

Tempest on Snake Island

Few theatre groups in the western world have done more in this field than Welfare State International. The integration of their theatre with the real nature of festival has been very successful. Carl Jung said that the timeless myths surface in our collective unconscious because they hold the answer to the secret mysteries of the universe. Welfare State replay these myths in sometimes the most obscure and esoteric way and yet, in contradiction to those in the arts world who contend that the ordinary person cannot appreciate art, produce wonderful theatre for all.

In 1981 Welfare State were invited to the Toronto Theatre Festival in Canada and I was invited to work with them. We arrived in Toronto knowing little about the project other than that it was based on *The Tempest*. I read through the play on the plane going over to Canada from Scotland and wondered why Welfare State had chosen a Shakespearian script. But as it turned out they took the themes in the play which were timeless and universal and turned them into a modern myth.

Toronto Festival is typical of the type of festival found in most major cities in the West. It is a collection of high quality international arts products mixed with a local input which usually constitutes a fringe. It is rare for festival organisers to see the huge potential of mobilising a large scale event which galvanises the city's own communities. The festival usually has little relationship with the general community in the city in which it is held. Festivals are not designed as festivals in the proper sense of the word but as a collection of international culture in a particular place.

Welfare State realised that as an overseas group being brought into this international venue they did not necessarily feel comfortable with the accepted arts

festival structure. They wanted to hold an event which
would link back to the community. They therefore
planned to hold their show on Snake Island which was
part of an archipelago which lies about two miles out
into the lake from Toronto where a community had
lived for some time. It gave the company a community
base and also a beautiful site for a performance It was
into this community that the company moved and lived
for the five weeks it took to build the show. The
audience would have to sail to it by ferry and so I
began to see the relevance of *The Tempest* which is of
course the story of a shipwreck on a lonely island.

The festival organisers were disturbed by the theatre
group who would not comply with the usual structures
and I remember John Fox, the co-artistic director, and
one of the organisers in an argument about the time we
were to start. John had wanted the show to start at
sunset and the organisers wanted 8.00pm put on the
ticket because no one would know when sunset was.
'That's my point', said John. 'It's incredible that we live
in a world whose inhabitants don't even know when the
sun goes down.'

At 8.00pm (or sunset) three of the company including
myself met the audience at the city pier where we
boarded the ferry and set off to cross the water to the
island. There were three characters on board. I was
playing a loud fairground showman called Hopper, who
acted as a sort of Prospero, a hunchback called Boris
who doubled as Caliban was played by John Bolton and
a strange washerwoman was played by Sue Gill. The
audience had started out on the journey in the usual
frame of mind, but after a while they began to see that
this was not going to be a normal theatre going
experience. Instead they were being led into the
unknown, just as Shakespeare's characters had been.

Although I was playing a sort of guide for the audience, the lights had failed on the dress rehearsal so I had no idea what was going to happen. We were all going on an adventure, the cast and the audience. We were leaving the world as we knew it to explore another. I realised that it was my responsibility to contribute my own feelings and thoughts. And so we arrived. Some of the cast and the children of the island were there to welcome us and played music at our arrival and we paraded along the pathways that connected the islands to the accompaniment of songs and dance in the fading light of dusk.

The first sight of Snake Island was beautiful. Lanterns and coloured lights illuminated the darkening night as we saw a crowd of strange characters playing a game which was a cross between tennis and croquet. It was like a scene out of Alice in Wonderland. The audience was led over a Japanese bridge onto the island itself. I knew they felt nervous, especially on the first night when people had dressed up in their theatre best. Gum boots and parkas would have been more appropriate. Although the audience felt quite physically safe they were disorientated. They were face to face with the night where sensations were awakened, instincts called upon and part of themselves that had long slept in the cradle of the city was brought back to life.

The two hundred people in the audience were asked to sit down on cut logs in a tight circle, shoulder to shoulder. There were no soft seats here where one could sit back and appraise the efforts of others; they were right in it. They were confused but also excited, because what is wonderful about Welfare State is that they respect their audience and, although they disorientate them, they do not abuse them.

The crowd were now in a tight circle as the drums started and the flaming lights were lit.

Lords and ladies, kings and babies ... I'm your life
I am everyman's destiny.
My hand is on your shoulder
tomorrow, today and yesterday;
I am the joker up your sleeve and the flea in your
   ear.

Boris Howarth,
Engineers of the Imagination, Coult and Kershaw

I then led them out of the circle and onto a path which
narrows into a small wood. The first night I did not
know what I would find there myself and as I entered I
could see the space filled with magically lit with owl-
shaped lanterns. I felt that I had entered a fairy wood.
Suddenly through the trees I could see Boris cowering
over an open fire in a small clearing. I felt that I was no
longer an actor in a play; it had all become real and I
was now looking at a lost soul in the dark. We called
each other's names across the wood as he vanished into
the night. I was shaken, as I am sure the audience were,
for the world of human misery and loss had suddenly
become alive in that small wood. By what seemed
spontaneous combustion, the real had become unreal
and the unreal real.

   The next part took place as the audience came out of
the trees. Thirty foot puppets and other images moved
amid the smoke and fireworks. The sound was loud
mystical music and the audience had moved from the
intimate to the spectacular. As this part was ending a
search light picked me up again and I led them onto a
small beach surrounded by woodland. The audience
were again in tight proximity and looked out to the
Toronto skyline of skyscrapers dominated by the
'Needle' observatory tower.

   Suddenly a rowing boat filled with skeletons towed an
effigy of the city skyline into view. John Fox, who was

wading in the water, put a flaming torch to it and the audience watched it burn. People started to clap and then to cheer. As the distant city in miniature burned there was a feeling of relief.

We went on past a lovely bower with children playing music and reached a warmly decorated area where the audience sat down to watch a shadow puppet play. Silhouettes of skeletons burned. Warm glasses of cider were passed around and the band struck up for a bush-cum-barn dance where cast and audience danced together, sharing the warmth of the moment.

The show was only half way through but the audience were already transformed by the range of experiences and exhilaration of the night. The form had transcended the mode of audience as critic and performer as provider. The theatre had become a theatre of the source, a festival for us all.

When the dance was over the audience were taken to a wedding and watched as a boat decorated with candles moved out to sea unaided. They were led down an avenue of lanterns by Death playing the bagpipes, paraded back to the ferry amid flaming torches and were sent on their way back to that other world of Toronto amid ceremony and music. Many people shook my hand as they left telling me it had been one of the most wonderful nights of their lives and I believed it had been.

It was a wonderful example of what a real festival can be for any community if they are willing to explore their own spirit and discover the real meaning behind our need to celebrate.

We can see how celebratory theatre might help us celebrate in the good times but what is celebratory theatres role when the community is going through crisis.

Festival in Disaster

On Ash Wednesday 1983 in Macedon, a rural community outside Melbourne, a huge bush fire completely destroyed the town and the surrounding environment. It was a terrible disaster with hundreds of houses and buildings being destroyed, eight people killed and dozens injured. The Ash Wednesday fires became headlines throughout the world and proved to be one of the worst natural disasters that Australia has experienced.

I was, on the night of the fire, watching a performance of Circus Oz in a circus tent which began to fill with smoke. The audience was evacuated at once and it was only then that we realised that the smoke was coming from Macedon which was fifty kilometres away. Although I felt sympathetic when I saw it in the newspaper I did not realise the true desolation caused by the fire.

Several weeks later I was at Arts Access talking to their executive officer, the indomitable Dinny Downie, when she received a call for someone to run some activities for the fire victims. Dinny was keen to see that something was done and this request led to the idea of running a theatre project. Fortunately the officer in charge of A.N.Z. Trustees, Vince Kiss, was willing to help. In express time he consulted with his trustees and we received some funding. More financial help came from the Victorian Department of Youth, Sport and Recreation whose director had seen the terrific morale boost entertainers had given the victims of the cyclone in Darwin.

While the funding was being organised we set about planning the project. I was at that time working with West Theatre Company and we felt that rather than perform for them it would be better to involve the people of Mt Macedon in a performance of their own. We went to the community to see if they in fact wanted to take a part in a project. One of the local aid committee, Judy Rose, gave me a chance to present the idea to the relevant committee of local people.

I was not prepared in any way for the sight of desolation that I found. The media accustoms us to disasters, but this was the first one that I had experienced in person. The scene resembled photographs of the First World War with the entire environment destroyed as far as the eye could see. The whole country was black and charred with the wrecks of hundreds of buildings scattered through the debris. There was not one bit of green in the scene and it looked as though there never would be again. The entire fabric of people's lives and community had been destroyed within an hour and now they were living in caravans as refugees. There were no animals and few birds to brighten the scene and for all intents and purposes it was a vision of the end of the world.

I arrived at the meeting and a long discussion ensued. The result was that we were given every encouragement by local people but the chances of success could not be guaranteed. Many locals and people from Melbourne were cynical as to the outcome.

But Judy Rose was undeterred and said that we must all give it a try and see what would happen.

It seemed to me that the only show likely to succeed was a celebration of the will to rebuild and a festival to show the strength of combined community action. The community must use the arts to express its pain, a catharsis to clear the way for new strength to emerge.

Winter had come and with it the rain and cold. The area around the caravans was a quagmire and the need to keep warm and dry in the flimsy caravans was a priority. Mental pressures were keen. People had lost a

lifetime of personal memories in a few minutes and as
one woman said to me, 'It's not the T.V. or the lounge
suite I care about. It's all my photographs and letters
that tell me who I am that matter.' With the destruction
of their environment people had lost the sense of
themselves. Also, relationships which had flourished in
a spacious house were now being pushed to breaking
point by the confines of a tiny caravan. The children too,
were suffering all the signs of trauma and some were
bursting into tears when a match was lit, let alone a real
fire. Some houses were saved due to freak winds or a
determined fight by the residents to save them and this
caused resentments and strained relations in the
community where some people still had their homes but
others didn't.

We were funded for three weeks of rehearsal towards
a one off event and as with other projects we decided
that we had to move into the area. Again Judy Rose
came to the rescue and organised for the company to
move into caravans and houses in the area or its
surrounds.

The first thing to do was to determine the form. There
were few buildings left in the area and certainly
nowhere big enough to perform inside, which left us
with the open air. As it was winter, a night performance
was out of the question because of the cold. So the form
was determined by the circumstances rather than by
choice. There was no stage and so we designed one on
the back of two forty foot haulage trailers which a local
contractor lent us. We were performing in a way as our
ancestors did on the back of carts, but this time on the
modern equivalent.

Next was a story or dramatic form on which to build
the theatre. I went back through old histories and
newspapers and discovered the area had experienced
disasters and difficulties in the past and it seemed that

this would be a good starting point. If we could show the community spirit that had faced problems in the past, the present difficulties might be easier to face.

The community had an interesting history.

Macedon had been discovered by the explorer, Major Mitchell in the 1830s. He had been an admirer of Alexander the Great and had named all the landmarks around the area after his hero. Alexander had come from Macedonia and therefore the name Macedon was coined. It is located on a large hill which is cooler in the summer and this attracted the administration to retire there, Indian-style, 19th century to escape the heat of Melbourne.

Melbourne society built summer mansions and English gardens and spent the summer months in quiet retreat. But the gold rush was on and the route to the gold mines ran close by and was busy with prospectors from all over the world. The gold was taken back from the goldfields to Melbourne by this route and the local woods were infested with bushrangers. The first fire hit in the late 1890s and destroyed much of the community and a number of country houses including the Governor's. The second major fire hit in what was to be called the Black Friday fires of 1939. Again the community was decimated.

All this was a base on which to start work and now we tried to recruit people to help. We started at the schools and they were very helpful as the children were suffering from the dislocation and obviously needed some positive activity. The young people jumped at the chance and started to build scenes and ideas. We also contacted other groups, individuals and networks to invite them to take part but although we were promised support there was little actual participation. One resident commented that it was a waste of time and money as no one wanted to celebrate a disaster.

We were based in a temporary shed that had been erected as a community centre after the fires but was not being used. We set up visual arts, drama and music and although the young people contributed, few of the adults came forward.

We began to think that the cynics had been right and the comment about no one wanting to help was true. We had been there sixteen days and there had been little response. There were only four days to go and I was seriously worried and felt that we had been wrong to attempt it.

However, on the Wednesday of the production week (the show was to be held on the Saturday) there was a sudden leap of interest. I have never been able to explain it but that morning we had all sorts of people calling in to offer help and support. It was really surprising; by the Saturday there were one hundred and ten people performing in the show.

It was a windy day which threatened rain but as it happened it stayed dry until ten minutes after the event. We had put up the stage in the pub car park, the pub being one of the few properties saved because it had been a refuge point for the people and had been defended by the fire fighters. About seven hundred people turned up and mixed freely with all the costumed performers. At two o'clock the audience were asked to process towards the school oval to see the start of the show. It was a great march as the people walked down the road together to music and drums. The feeling of community had already started to assert itself as the audience and cast surrounded the empty oval. Suddenly a helicopter that had been used for fire fighting came over the top of the mount and landed on the oval. The 'ghost' of Major Mitchell and his wife had returned to help the community in their time of need. They disembarked and led the audience to the stage.

Here Major Mitchell met a disgruntled family who were just about to move away from the area because it was all too much. He and his wife persuaded the family to give them a chance to show them what a fighting spirit is. The show unfolded with the struggles and the events that marked the lives of the people that have lived here before. Songs and dances punctuated the show and after an hour of past adventures we reached the more serious climax.

A sixty foot long fire dragon arrived with fire and smoke, worked by eleven puppeteers, and in a mad dance destroyed a beautiful bird. It then mounted the stage in a victory dance. The audience suddenly heard bells in the distance and the fire fighters who fought the real fire arrived in their engine. They leapt off to fight the dragon which was subdued and killed. It's head was cut open and its blood, which was represented by two hundred red helium balloons, poured into the sky. The local doctor pronounced it dead.

The community had won and the whole cast came silently onto stage. Major Mitchell and his wife, who had been the narrators, asked the family if they were going to stay. They told him they would think again and joined the cast for the final song.

Then followed one of the most powerful moments I have experienced in this type of theatre.

The cast sang a song of victory over the fire and their determination to rise again. As they sang, the bird which had been killed arose out of the ashes to be a phoenix of rebirth. At the same time the cast held up banners and signs which they had erected in their burnt out homes: WE WILL SURVIVE or ROSES WILL BLOOM AGAIN swayed above the actors. The effect on the audience was electrifying and people started to cry with grief for what they had lost but also at the beauty of the human will to fight back. There was no separation of performer or audience and no separate identities: the community stood as one.

The moment the song was finished the kids attacked the dragon which had been laid out on the ground behind the stage. They literally tore it to bits in a frenzy of laughter and joy. In minutes there was little of it left. The children had had their revenge.

Macedon was a festival and a celebration and the message was clear. We must in all celebrations touch the centre of our feelings about life and each other and the situations in which we find ourselves. We must allow our artists a chance to use their skills to bring back meaning and mystery into our festivals and celebrations. Theatre must be allowed to return to its roots.

Local Festivals

There has been a huge increase in the number of local festivals in the last ten years and it is rare not to find one in the local area. These very often have the same format and do not necessarily involve the professional arts. But when they involve experienced festival artists the effect can be startling, producing new ways of holding events, deepening the meaning of those events and having a massive increase in audience numbers.

Fire on the Water

In 1988 in Darwin there was an evening market held on a beautiful tropical beach. It was a wonderful experience to go down there at sunset and walk between the dozens of open stalls lit with lanterns and lamps and select your food from cultures from all over the world. Filipino, Sri Lankan, French, African, Thai, Malaysian came to sell their food. As well, stalls display all sorts of colourful wares for sale and jugglers, musicians and actors perform regularly. Thousands of Darwin people went there every Thursday to eat and enjoy the atmosphere. It is hard to define why a particular spot feels good to us; all we know is that when we are there we feel calm and better within ourselves.

It was an obvious place to hold an event during Darwin's annual Bougainvillea Festival. There was a ready made audience but it was also a place with a special feeling that we wanted to explore. The festival organisers wanted to transcend the normal festival program and produce something which would start to engage the deeper feelings that festivals must tap if they are to call themselves celebrations.

We decided to build large images at sea which would float above the water as the sun went down and amid ceremony, parades, fireworks and music, they would be burnt. Ken Conway, the director of Brown's Mart Community Theatre, came up with an idea to use as an artistic base for the project: the life and work of artist Ian Fairweather. He lived in Darwin in 1953 and, so the story goes, was inspired by the Kon Tiki expeditions to sail from Darwin to Timor and thereby prove that Aboriginal people could have done so. He was fascinated by the fact that, apart from some Macassan traders who came to Australia to get sea cucumbers, there was no evidence that the Aboriginal people had had any contact with the outside world. Fairweather wanted to prove that it was possible for the contact to have been made and proceeded to build a raft from some old second world war petrol tanks to make the journey. He set out without proper provisions and within an hour lost his rudder. He was forced to lie down on the deck to keep the craft stable and within three days his food ran out. The journey of two hundred and fifty miles took eleven days and he was eventually washed up on the shores of the island of Roti. He was then arrested as a spy and imprisoned for several weeks! His painting style was greatly changed by his adventures and the delirious visions he had seen.

We constructed huge images based on the paintings done after his journey, hoping to capture his visions and hallucination. These were to be mounted on the beach below the high tide line so that the water would act as a natural barrier to the crowd during the event. A burning sun, shrieking horses riding clouds of black smoke, snaking Aboriginal crocodiles, masklike faces, were all made up by local artists and students. We used bamboo and wire fames with paper mache coverings which, as well as being large and strong, were super light. There was good reason for this. The tides in Darwin reach seven metres and to raise the images above them we had to build frames over thirty foot high which would be able to withstand the tides coming in and out.

We carried the images down to the sand and waited until the sea went out. We had only four hours to put up the images before the tide came in. Ropes were tied to the frames with a four wheel drive to pull them and with the help of the arts team and several bemused bathers we pulled them up. We finished our work as the water lapped our feet. We sat above the high tide line and watched nervously as the tide rose up to eighteen feet. But the images stood firm and swayed gently in the breeze.

The next evening ten thousand people gathered to see the event. They had eaten at the market and sat to watch the sun set behind the images. As darkness fell a parade of fiery torches, masks and a forty foot gecko puppet built by artist Tim Newth led the firelighters to their boat. Bowmen released two hundred fiery arrows as a twenty piece metal drum band played African rhythms.

We had rigged the images with fireworks and we sailed out to sea to light them. Silver fountains, catherine wheels, fire, smoke and rockets brought the images to life and reflections turned the sea to fire. I was filled with a strange emotion and I realised that the audience and images had created a feeling that was rarely found in today's society: it was a wonderful and powerful affirmation of life's wonder and power.

It was only later that I discovered that the event and the market were situated on a powerful Aboriginal dreamline. These lines cross and recross Australia and depict the journeys of the mythical creatures who created our land in Aboriginal belief. The line was not just generally going through the area but exactly through the images. Mindil beach was also an Aboriginal burial ground. We had instinctively found a spot that had been used for thousands of years by Aboriginal people for ceremonial purposes.

John Arden summed up these feelings in his account of a festival in India.

The dances went on all night until dawn broke. I fell asleep at one point and dreamt dreams of battles and murders to the rhythm of the drums—at intervals I half awoke and saw through bleary eyes the same continuous stamping up and down of proud spangled giants, waving their spears and threatening each other with their arrows. From beginning to end the noise was enormous. I was not the only person in the audience who fell asleep—it did not matter. The gods were there and their power was in the village, whether the people slept or woke. They had been called up and they had arrived.

The Sports Festival

Just as ceremonies work in local communities they can also work in national and international context where a whole culture can celebrate itself and bring about new national identity.

As I write this the Olympic Games are being held in Spain. They have become truly a world event. They have brought the world together into a single, readily identifiable unit and in spite of the commercialism, the political pressures and the huge amounts of money involved, they have become a symbol of human unity. They have brought the countries together in competition but still maintaining good will. However, it is not in the competition but in the Opening and Closing Ceremonies that we can witness, for better or worse, a world event in the true meaning of the word.

Some countries have treated these ceremonies as a huge chance to promote a shallow razzamattaz, but others have seen the opportunity to show a vision on a huge scale of human harmony. Who could forget the Seoul Olympics ceremony with eighty thousand lanterns and a view of the Milky Way.

Artists have a unique chance to become involved in these types of events to show a massive audience a vision of a human unity. In Australia this medium has hardly evolved. All too often when we have a chance to show our culture to a mass audience at sporting events the results have been lamentable. The organisers of who have often done a superb job in pulling together a large scale event have little to no experience in dealing with artists and artists who could organise wonderful ceremonies do not know how to work within sports structures. Yet if these two disparate worlds are brought together the results can focus a truly Australian feeling with which we can be proud to identify.

In Darwin, artists have been experimenting with this very theme and the results have been very interesting and exciting. The Northern Territory has played host to two international sporting events which have invited many countries to participate. However, the organisers have had the vision to strive to hold an event which would symbolise a new unity between people. I should like to describe one of them to show the huge potential that lies beneath the surface of our community.

The Arafura Games

The Northern Territory Government invited nine countries from South East Asia and the Pacific region to participate in a sports festival in Darwin in 1990. They wanted to stage an Opening Event which would truly reflect the Territory's unique culture and also show respect for our neighbouring countries.

The event was held at night in Darwin's then largest sports arena with a stage in the centre. Twelve thousand people came to watch. As the sun set, Aboriginal music hummed an explosion of energy through the huge speaker system and two elders from Arnhem Land came onto the oval and danced their welcome. Far from seeming small in that large area, the men filled the ground with their presence as they sat down to light a fire using only two sticks. This simple act of firelighting which all of our ancestors have used throughout time to survive, brought home to all watching, the link between us all in past time. As the small fire burst into life there was a huge cheer by the audience. The flame was transformed to a firebrand and carried in honour across the field. The elders had started the event in the 'proper way' and now the flame was ready to bring the Games alight. Students with twenty foot flags followed the flame around the area and in their turn brought on a parade of a thousand lanterns. Several hundreds of local children had worked with artists and teachers for many weeks to produce a lantern for each child made in the shape of a Northern Territory animal. It was an awe inspiring sight as nearly a half a kilometre of beautiful images paraded around the oval, which was otherwise in darkness, forming a hugh spiral. Music written for the event built slowly until all the lanterns were inside the oval and gave a real feeling of the power of the land in which the event was taking place.

Now the countries marched in to live music from their homelands. Each team was led by a thirty foot lantern of the animal that represented their country. Local Darwin people from those countries carried the lanterns or walked alongside, playing music, drumming and dancing, dressed in the fabulous costumes which are their national dress. Australia entered last to a cheer that was heartfelt for the land we live in. Gone was the hard edge of aggressive competition and the false rhetoric of national sentimentality and in its place was a sense of true celebration, a celebration about what makes us different and what makes us the same and, definitely, a new awareness of what it meant to live in Darwin as Australians. Two Aboriginal elders led the team of eight hundred into the grounds to the sound of the didgeridoo and behind came a huge rock wallaby carried by twelve people and glowing with a beautiful translucent light.

The potential for these events, following the principles of celebratory theatre, is enormous. In Australia it is also a chance to show a very large number of people the real feelings and culture of the oldest land on earth.

PARADES

Another form which celebratory theatre can positively transform is the parade. Parades may be split into three main types.

The first is the political march, where people will gather together to show their strong feelings about a particular issue. This act of walking to demonstrate one's commitments brings about a sense of purpose and resolve that the act of standing still in a crowd does not. Perhaps it is the sense of movement and of travelling to a destination that brings about this feeling and, like all journeys, the going can be more exciting than the arrival. Perhaps it is the feeling of action, or participation, the feeling of everyone being on an equal footing that makes each individual feel worthwhile in spite of the large numbers that are often involved. There is usually no formal audience to stand and watch the march; the emphasis is on being a participant. It is always a terrific feeling to present theatre at such an event where music, songs, large images and plays can focus the feeling of optimism and resolve.

The second type of parade is the street procession where in the English speaking countries at least, there are participants and an audience to watch. There are usually 'floats' which are trucks which are decorated to form some kind of display, with people also arranged on them. The word 'float' might have come from the great river parades of the eighteenth century, where huge decorated boats used to float down the Thames. Our modern version is for the floats to line up in daylight and make their way down the main streets accompanied by brass bands and various local clubs and groups. But they have become, in our culture, events 'for the kids' and like our modern festivals have lost a great deal of their potential.

The important reason for having a festival is often forgotten and repetition takes over—'it happened last year so it should happen again'. The formula is repeated until it is a shell empty of inner meaning. The big city parades are often sponsored by large companies who, once again, supplant community awareness and involvement with what are often no more than rolling ads for television coverage.

The third type of parade is a minority group declaring its views. In Australia the Gay Mardi Gras parade in Sydney is interesting. It is an excellent example of a minority group 'coming out' for a brilliant display for one night a year and being recognised. It is a wonderful display of costume and visual spectacle, full of excitement and energy. This can often be the formula for creative spectaculars. They have only one night of glory and therefore put everything into it. The Romans changed place with their slaves for one night a year and the Festival of Fools in medieval France allowed thieves and beggars to 'rule' for a day. The wonderful West Indian parades in London, where participants spend all year making the most spectacular of costumes, are a recent example. Each individual has something to say in a creative way and they march through the streets together to say it.

Great Parades

The great parades of South America, where the Mardi Gras is held; or India, where millions gather to share a celebration of their beliefs; or the fantastic floats of Viareggio in Italy, which are so large and spectacular that is hard to believe they are real; the Fallas in Valencia in Spain where huge and beautiful structures are burnt all over the city, should bring into question the emptiness of the ordinary parades in Britain and

Australia. The are pale imitations of what is possible if the community and artists take them seriously. It is sad to see so much of our artistic energy going into galleries and theatres when such exiting, popular, artistically challenging and financially viable alternatives are waiting to be picked up.

Street processions need not be held in the day and, in transferring them to the night, can bring about a whole new world of magic and expression. I think of the Japanese festivals where large floats move along the streets as images of beauty and mystery, with thousands of coloured lanterns and flaming torches: a sight to remember for life. They need not have motorised vehicles at all.

Getting rid of the idea of floats sometimes can be very effective. It changes an event to be watched to an event which people are in, walking all together shoulder to shoulder.

Darwin Trade Union Parade

In 1918 there was an uprising in Darwin. The local people overthrew the Administrator who was then the governor of the region. He had made many unfortunate and high handed decisions which had enraged the local people. He finally sealed his fate by nationalising the pubs and putting up the price of beer! The Trade Unions led the march on Government House and burnt an effigy of the Administrator outside. He barricaded himself inside the building until a gunboat came to get him out.

The Trade Unions in Darwin had traditionally held their parades on May Day but during recent years the attendance had fallen off. They wanted to revitalise their parade and felt the arts could help. It was 1988 and re-enacting the past was being done all over the country

for the Bicentennial year. As the unions had led the
storming of Government House they felt this was a
relevant subject for re-enactment. They applied for
funds and I was to take on the job with my then work
partner Jan (Meme) McDonald.

It is vital that all re-enactments be carefully
approached. It is not just a matter of dressing up in
period costumes and walking through the event. This
does not produce a feeling of history in an audience but
a slightly awkward embarrassment. Theatre which is
going to use an historical incident for its base must
relate to the feeling of its present audience in order to
become meaningful. The first decision was to make sure
that the parade was on foot with no floats. This would
give everyone a feeling of participation and physically
put everyone at the same level.

The arts team built, with the help of unionists, six
sixteen foot puppets, a moveable thirty foot effigy,
hundreds of red flags, a steel drum band and new
banners. The parade was to march to Government
House with colour, music, huge symbols and a feeling
of festival. The present Administrator agreed to act the
part of his infamous predecessor and the scene was set.

At ten o'clock in the morning thousands of people
gathered to storm the government. The union
movement had become excited about what was
happening. It was more than a march now. It had
become an activity that promised to be fun and had
meaning to people; the idea appealed. We all live with
the feeling that governments control our lives in too
many ways. It also gave the participants the feeling that
in times of real oppression the people's voice must be
listened to.

We wanted to encourage a feeling that we really did
have control of our lives and the democratic process.
The speeches of the actors reflected the feelings we all

have in the face of oppression, which are as true today as at the time. The climax to the show was the burning of the thirty foot effigy which symbolised the forces of injustice. The audience felt empowered and satisfied. The Trade Union Parade had taken a new form and the people had responded in their thousands. The idea of unionism was kept intact with the idea of oppression being overthrown and collective action being effective. The artistic and the political had emerged into a feeling of community strength.

River Parade

West Theatre was asked to hold an event for the one hundred and fiftieth year of the founding of the State of Victoria. We believed that we should attempt to produce an event that reflected some of the feelings stated above. The idea evolved into a parade, but it would be held on the River Yarra as a finish to a festival being held on its banks. I believe that it was a courageous decision by the organiser, Mark Avery, to attempt something which had a high risk factor but might bring something original to the celebrations.

We were able to find boats of all descriptions ranging from forty ton barges to small nineteenth century whaling boats, from beautiful launches to little steam boats and even a Maltese gondola. The real problem was the subject matter. It is vital that events have a real feeling to express.

One of the people concerned in the year's celebration said that Victorian culture could be represented in a river parade by a huge pie with children on it, a football with the champion team sitting in it and a beer can with dancing girls around it. We disagreed with this most wholeheartedly. This attitude seemed to totally miss the point of real celebration and to have the lowest opinion of people's capacity to feel anything deeply. We felt the idea to be much more complex than that.

It is difficult to celebrate an historical landmark in a culture that has injured another without that celebration being an affront to the indigenous people. One of the team, John Lane, went to see a group of Aboriginal people to ask them what they thought we should do. They said that first there was harmony, then the whites came and there was blood and pain, then there was mechanisation and disease and then, he hesitated, and said slowly, 'And I hope there will be harmony again.' We felt that it was important to reflect these ideas in the parade.

The parade became a representation of the four seasons of rhythmic change that affect all of our lives but we built in another season which we called Spring Again, which symbolised the hope for harmony in the future.

Thirty seven craft were decorated with symbols for the seasons: Spring, which included a huge barge with a sixteen foot Earth Mother with dancers and singers; Summer, whose main image was a twenty foot sun rigged with fireworks; Autumn, with several images of old age and maturity; and Winter, which was a spectacular vision of Death, constructed on a derelict ship. These were accompanied by dozens of smaller boats with all sorts of effects, fireworks, flames, music and large scale puppets. It was the first time we had organised a parade on the water. When we lined the boats up the entire length was over half a kilometre.

We learnt a good deal that night. Most of our education was about water and its particular problems. Communications, lights and sound are all very complex in that sort of environment, when there is no chance to rehearse beforehand.

The management of the three hundred people helping needs a huge amount of organisation and expertise, especially at night on a river. Some of the images did not work as they were either too small or too unstable in a water environment. But the river had given a great magic to the events. Huge suns exploding in fireworks, rockets being fired from a barge with two hundred paper lanterns decorating it, large shadow puppets lit with naked torches passing in the night, a huge barge of Death, filled with images and, on the shore opposite the audience, a line of two hundred people holding up flaming torches in a triumphant conclusion.

The potential of this sort of event is unlimited and can form the basis of new forms of procession.

RITUALS

The third type of celebration is the private event which we practiced throughout the world which is usually to celebrate a happy event such as a wedding or a solemn one, such as a funeral. The people of the English speaking world find it harder and harder to celebrate even in the context of their private lives. These ceremonies are no longer brought out into the community but take place in relative seclusion.

Our funerals, for example, are now hidden away and it is rare to actually see one. The whole event is organised with the minimum of personal involvement and is almost clinical and antiseptic in its approach. The service is often fitted into a tight schedule to last a prescribed amount of time and is the same for each group. The music, or should I call it 'muzak', is inspired and the coffin slips away behind a curtain on a little track as if it is on its way to a railway station. Mourners are deprived of a meaningful ceremony which allows them to express their emotions. But people are reacting to the lack of meaning in our rituals and are now using their own creativity and symbolism to bring back meaning into the milestones in our personal lives.

People can take control of their own ceremonies and design them to their own needs. Artists and musicians can help the lay person plan and hold events which are meaningful for them. However the system already in place such as undertaker services and registry offices are not designed for events which deviate from the norm. It is important to get legal advice and to check what is possible within the legal structure. Namings and marriages are now being held by celebrants who are usually pleased to work with the participants to deepen the meaning for them. Funerals can be very difficult to influence. There is sometimes little to no warning about the death of someone close and people are grieved and find it difficult to cope with the problems of designing a more personalised service.

Yet I believe that all these services evolved because we need to go through an event which gives a focus for our feelings at times of great personal importance. These ceremonies have been developed over tens of thousands of years and are designed in certain ways because they help the spiritual and intellectual parts of ourselves come to terms with what is happening either in joy or sadness. It is dangerous to the health of a society to allow these personal events to deteriorate in meaning, thereby bypassing the real feelings of expression and leaving people unresolved and confused.

Some people might say that these ceremonies are the province of the religious professionals and that artists have no part to play in the area of personal ceremony. I believe that it is not the artist's role to determine what the content of the event should be. That it is the work of the people who are holding the event. Rather the adults should use their techniques to help deepen people's feelings in a personally meaningful way.

Drama Action—A Personal Ritual

Drama Action is a theatre centre in Sydney which for many years was run by a devoted and woman called Bridget Brandon. I have worked there many times and have taught ritual theatre, but the students took me by surprise when at the end of a show they took me through a ritual of their own. We had produced 'Inanna,' the ancient Sumerian tale, one of the oldest stories on earth, and the next day had finished our debriefing. The director of any piece of theatre is often placed alone in the process of theatre making and isolated from the rest of the team. The job requires one to remain detached and objective, but after a show is over the same position often prevails. The students at Drama Action had recognised this and constructed a ritual to show me how they felt. I had no idea of what was going to happen and was about to leave the students for the last time. They blindfolded me and lay me on the floor. They picked me up horizontally on their shoulders and took me outside to a place in the gardens. I had no idea where I was going and felt very vulnerable. But I trusted the students and decided to let go of all expectations and allow myself the experience. I was carefully put down on some soft grass and I could smell flowers. I felt each student put their hands on my body and with a group of 45 it was a moving experience to feel the energy of ninety hands on my being. The students sang a song and slowly left until I could only hear the singing in the distance. I lay suspended in time in a state of deep emotion. When I opened my eyes I was in a lovely garden and around my body, in a circle, were forty little clay figures of the Goddess Inanna made by the students.

****

A Special Artist

In all the examples given the artists who succeed in this environment have to have special experience. In all forms of theatre there are specialists and Celebratory theatre of this type is no exception. This is often confusing to festival and events organisers as they usually make no distinction between one kind of artist and another, yet to involve the wrong sort of specialist in this area can produce bad results. It is vital that universities and colleges identify this specialist branch of theatre and make allowance for it in their courses. It is a field which has a lot of employment potential and demands a high degree of talent and skill. I hope that we see in Australia a new movement which gives the potential events artists a chance to train in the right way and can give the quality needed if this vital form of human activity is to thrive.

Conclusion

There is a grave danger that in developing greater sophistication a society can move away from shared meaning. A sophisticated arts structure does not necessarily indicate cultural richness. A rich culture is one in which the arts express people's understanding and beliefs as part of their lives.

In many western societies who public and personal rituals and festivals are so empty of meaning. Our public festivals and celebrations, our parades and our private rituals are being strangled by commercialism, mediocrity and habit. The meaning behind our community, in the widest use of that word, is being trivialised by government and business interests. We are losing control of our own symbolism and, if we are to keep our freedom, we must defend it with resolve and use it to bring about a feeling of self worth and power. Theatre has no small part to play in allowing this to happen. Arts history and traditions have always, until recent times anyway, been intimately involved in festival, parade and celebration. The modern separation is, I feel, damaging our culture and it is now time to bring about their reintegration.

AFTERWORD

■

A Look to
the Future

*People say that what we're all seeking is a meaning
to life. I don't think that's what we're really seeking.
I think what we're seeking is the experience of being
alive, so that our life experiences on the purely
physical plane will have resonances within our
innermost being and reality, so that we actually feel
the rapture of being alive.*

JOSEPH CAMPBELL
The Power of Myth

As we reach the end of this millennium there are many
cultural futures open to us in Australia. Ever increasing
electronic entertainment is now dominating the patterns
of people's lives. The video age is upon us. Our children
are being born into a world where the means of
communication is so sophisticated that Marshall
McLuhan's global village has become a reality.
Individual cultures are now slowly merging into larger
and larger units with fewer and fewer differences.
Television, radio and newspapers are controlled by
fewer people and are often dominated by commercial

forces. Christianity, the principal influence on our western culture for nearly two thousand years, has now lost much of that power and our spiritual world is strangely in limbo. The world is in extreme danger from nuclear weapons and environmental damage threatens our fundamental existence.

As we probe deeper and deeper into science, extending our knowledge in every direction, we find that our lives are becoming more and more complex. Our technical aids can extend our capacities in almost any direction yet the political and commercial systems which rule much of our lives are often self seeking.

The decisions about the world's future often lie in the hands of the people least qualified to make them.

But on a social level our world community is realising that we must change our fundamental relationship to each other if we are to survive. East and West are coming closer to co-operating and ending the struggle of the last few decades. Women and men have restructured their basic working relationship in ways that will produce a new generation which will have very different attitudes from their parents. Our political systems are changing to cope with the new demands for a better environment and a more equitable system.

In other words, we are in the midst of a huge cultural upheaval. We must keep sight of those things which are important to us as individuals and as a community. One of those things is our creativity.

We need to be able to live in a world which is not mono-cultural and we must not let ourselves be turned into passive consumers of culture. We must develop strong cultural roots which feed us with understanding and strength. These roots must supply and nourish a creative flowering which means something to us all.

Community theatre has an important role to play. I believe that it has the power to liberate the human potential to communicate, celebrate and express feelings, concerns and visions that are the very foundation of human existence. While theatre is confined in its present structures it allows only a small, group of people access to it and this must be changed. Theatre must go back to the community.

We are at a cross road. In one direction lies a culture of ever increasing passive consumerism and in the other, a people's culture which allows participation, access and meaningful expression.

Can there be any doubt about which road we should follow?

> *Lookout, lookout, I'm the lookout man*
> *Listen to my song*
> *I'm the Ballad Monger*
> *But I cannot sing for long*
> *And I sing of right and wrong...*
>
> *Tonight you lose your lover*
> *Tonight the banks will sink*
> *Tonight the ghosts of ghosts arise*
> *Tonight we're at the brink*

Song by John Fox

A SELECT BIBLIOGRAPHY

∎

ARTAUD, ANTONIN, *The Theatre and Its Double*, London: John Calder, 1977.

BOLTON, REG, *New Circus*, London: Calouste Gulbenkian Foundation, 1987.

BROCKETT, OSCAR G., *History of the Theatre*, Massachussets: Allyn and Bacon, 1987.

BROOK, PETER, *The Empty Space*, Harmondsworth: Penguin, 1972.

BURTON, PETER and LANE, JOHN, *New Directions, Ways of Advance for the Amateur Theatre*, London: MacGibbon and Kee, 1970.

CAMPBELL, JOSEPH, *The Power Of Myth*, Doubleday, 1988.

COULT & KERSHAW, *Engineers of the Imagination: The Welfare State Handbook*, London: Methuen, 1983.

DAVIS, R. G., *The San Francisco Mime Troupe: The First Ten Years*, Palo Alto: Ramparts Press, 1975.

FOTHERINGHAM, RICHARD, *Community Theatre in Australia*, Sydney: Currency Press, 1992.

GOOCH, STEVE, *All Together Now*, London: Methuen, 1984.

GROTOWSKI, JERZY, *Towards a Poor Theatre*, London: Methuen, 1975.

HARWOOD, RONALD, *All the World's a Stage*, London: Secker and Warburg, 1984.

HUNT, ALBERT, *Hopes for Great Happenings*, London: Methuen, 1976.

KELLY, OWEN, *Community, Art and the State*, Comedia.

LAEUCHLE, SAMUEL, *Religion and Art in Conflict*, Fortress Press.

MUNK, ERIKA (ed.), 'Theatre in Asia' *Drama Review*, (New York), 15:3 (T 50) Spring 1971.

NEIDJIE, BIG BILL, DAVIS, STEPHEN and FOX, ALLAN, *Australia's Kakadu Man*, Resource Managers', 1986.

PLIMPTON, GEORGE, *Fireworks: A History and Celebration* New York: Doubleday, 1984.

POWNALL, DAVID, *God Perkins*, London: Faber and Faber, 1977.

QUILICI, FOLCO, *Magic*, Bay Books.

ROOSE-EVANS, JAMES, *Experimental Theatre from Stanislavsky to Peter Brook*, London: Routledge and Kegan Paul, 1984.

SCHECHTER, JOEL, *Durov's Pig, Clowns, Politics and Theatre*, New York: Theatre Communications Group, 1985.

SNELL, GORDON (ed.), *The Book of Theatre Quotes, Notes Quotes and Anecdotes of the Stage*, London: Angus and Robertson, 1982

WILLETT, JOHN (ed.), *Brecht on Theatre*, New York: Hill and Wang, 1964

WYETH, CHRIS and KAREN, *Festival and Offbeat Events in Australia*, Kenthurst, Australia: Kangaroo Press, 1992.

Acknowledgements

The publishers gratefully acknowledge permission to produce extracts from the following publications:Sue Fox from *Engineers of the Imagination* Coult and Kershaw, *Methuen* London; *The San Francisco Mime Troupe* R. G. Davis *Ramparts Press*, Palo Alto; *Australia's Kakadu Man*, Neidjie, Davis, Fox, *Resource Managers*, Darwin; *Experimental Theatre from Stanislavsky to Peter Brook*, James Roose-Evans, *Routledge Kegan Paul*, London; *New Directions* Burton and Lane, *McGibbon Kee*, London; *All the World's a Stage* Ronald Harwood, *Secker & Warburg* London; 'Theatre in Asia' John Arden *Drama Review*, New York; Song by John Fox *Welfare State International*, Ulverstone; *The Book of Theatre Quotes* Gordon Snell, *Angus & Robertson* London, *Brecht on Theatre* (ed) John Willett, *Methuen*, London